Mātṛka Goddess Vaiṣṇavī

Mātṛka Goddess Vaiṣṇavī

Dr. Sanjaya Kumar Mahapatra

AAYU

AAYU PUBLICATIONS

New Delhi-110086

Cataloging in Publication Data--DK

Courtesy: D.K. Agencies (P) Ltd. <docinfo@dkagencies.com>

Mahapatra, Sanjaya Kumar, 1963- **author.**
Mātṛka goddess Vaiṣṇavī / Dr. Sanjaya Kumar Mahapatra. -- First edition.
pages cm
Includes bibliographical references and index.
ISBN 9789385161803

1. Vaiṣṇavī (Hindu deity)--Cult--India. 2. Vaiṣṇavī (Hindu deity)--Cult--India--Odisha. 3. Mother goddesses--Cult--India. 4. Mother goddesses--Cult--India--Odisha. 5. Vaiṣṇavī (Hindu deity)--In art. 6. Hindu art. I. Title.

LCC BL1225.V34M34 2018 | DDC 294.52114 23

Published by:

AAYU PUBLICATIONS
D-134, Agar Nagar, Prem Nagar-III
New Delhi-110086
Tel: 09910728725, 09654504227
Email: aayupublication@gmail.com
www.aayupublications.com

Mātṛka Goddess Vaiṣṇavī

First Edition 2018

ISBN: 978-93-85161-80-3

PRINTED IN INDIA

Printed at Unitech Graphic Point, Delhi

PREFACE

Saktism, the concept of Śakti, the source of all energies of the Universe plays a vital role in the religious tradition of India since the dawn of human civilization. Originated from the primitive mother goddess cult prevalent among the aboriginal society, Saktism gradually assimilated various heterogeneous traits and finally emerged as an independent religious thought forming a significant aspect of mainspring of Indian religious system. Unlike other religious sects, Saktism has a continuous and colourful history of its own. Although Saktism crept into other religions as the energizing power of male divinities, it has close affinity to Śaivism and has conceptualized that the procreation is possible only through the union of Śiva with Śakti.

The antiquity of Śakti cult in India dates back most probably to the 3rd millennium B.C. on the basis of terracotta figurines discovered from the Harappan sites and the historic rock shelters where the Śakti is manifested in triangular genital forms or in the forms of fecundity and fertility. She was invoked and adored in the names of Usā, Aditī, Śrī, Sarasvatī etc in the Vedic age while Durgā, Caṇḍikā, Saptamātṛkā, Yoginis, Cāmuṇḍā etc in the Epic and Mahābhārata periods. She is Mahākālī, Mahālakṣmī and Mahāsarasvatī as delineated in the Mārkaṇḍeya Purāṇa. Even modern Indian saints like Ramakṛsna Paramahamsa and Śrī Aurovinda have invoked this Śakti in the shape of Divine Mother. She is also regarded as the Māyā and Prakṛti by the Vedantins.

Being the primordial energy she creates, sustains and dissolves the universe. That is why since the dawn of civilization the worship of the Divine Mother crept into the spiritual and religious beliefs of mankind.

The Śakti cult occupies a pivotal position in the socio-religious life of Indian people. The paintings and engravings of the rock-cut art, the bisected triangles, the perforated stones in the rock shelters and the Yoni stone etc have not only strengthened the above statement but also provided the concrete materials to the scholars to prove the beginning of Śakti cult in India since the pre-historic period. Further, the primitive tree-worship is no doubt the early manifestation of mother-worship which reinforces the genesis of Śakti cult in India to a hoary past.

A band of female divinities entitled as Mātṛkās occupy an eminent place in the Hindu perception. They assume paramount significance especially in the goddess-oriented Tantric sect of Hinduism. These little Mothers are the endowed energies of the important familiar male deities. Early references to the Mātṛkās can be assigned to the first century A.D· as mentioned by David Kinsley .but they rarely specify their number, the implication in some passages is that they are innumerable. In the medieval period their number and names become more standardized. They are usually said to the number seven as Saptamātṛkās though some texts mention eight and sixteen. Since they are generally depicted as heptads, they are called Saptamātṛkās who in the Vedas form one band and take their seat on a moving chariot symbolized as the human body or each solar ray or each octave sound. Brahmāṇī or Sarasvatī, Māheśvarī or Raudrī, Kaumārī or Kātyāyanī, Vaiṣṇavī or Lakṣmī, Vārāhī, Indrāṇī or Māhendri and Cāmuṇḍā .are regarded as Saptamātṛkās symbolizing the incarnation of the supreme reality. However, they may sometimes be eight as Aṣṭamātṛkās. In South India the seven female divinities are worshipped under Saptamātṛkā *upāsanā* whereas the Aṣṭamātṛkās are venerated in Nepal .The Mātṛkās are a collective of seven or eight goddesses, whose paradoxical natures express the interrelationship between the cyclical nature of women's bodies and perennial earth based rituals. They are Mother Goddesses, yet not restricted to the procreative implication of motherhood. The Mātṛkās are aspects of the Great Goddess in her full power and work together in collective form. In the Devī-Mahātmya myth, they appear as aspects of the Great Goddess Durgā's power, which She calls forth to aid her in the battle against the asuras, demons. They spring from Durgā's forehead riding animal mounts (goose, bull, tiger, etc.) in their most terrifying forms and successfully restore equilibrium to the threatened cosmos.

Vaiṣṇavī is the counter part of Vishnu. She is depicted with four hands being seated upon a lotus, under a *rājavrikṣa*. She is dark in complexion with lovely face and pretty eyes. She wears a bright yellow garment. Her head is adorned with *kirīṭa-mukuṭa*. She is richly decorated with ornaments generally worn by Viṣṇu. She wears the *vanamāla*, the garland of Viṣṇu. The emblem on her banner as well as her *vāhana* is Garuda. When depicted with four arms, she carries in one of her hands the *cakra* and in the corresponding left hand the śaṅkha; her two other hands are held in the *abhaya* and the *varada mudrā* as described in the *Devī Purāṇa* and *Pūrvakaraṇāgama*.

The goddess Vaiṣṇavī, one of the benign aspects of the Divine Mother, has been described both as a Mātṛkā and Yoginī in the Indian literature. She is invariably displayed in the Saptamātṛkā panels hailing from various archaeological sites of India. It is proposed to furnish a short account of prominent Vaiṣṇavī images found elsewhere the sub-continent which will enrich the cultural heritage and sculptural art of India. It is to be noted that the sculptors of our land have presented the Vaiṣṇavī images starting from four-armed to the variety of six-armed. In this book an humble attempt has been made to survey the extant Vaiṣṇavī images of India which will shed light on the developmental aspect of iconic motifs.

The present treatise is comprised of seven chapters. Chapter One deals with the meaning, significance, genesis and evolution of Saktism in different stages. Chapter Two deals with the genesis, metaphysical significance and mythology of the goddess Mātṛkā. Chapter Three contains the general iconography of Mātṛkās with special reference to the iconography of Vaiṣṇavī images. Chapter Four provides the detailed accounts of the sculptural representation of Mātṛkās in Indian as well as in Odishan context. Chapter Five sheds light on the interpretation of the Vaiṣṇavī images surveyed during the course of research work. Chapter Six deals with the ritualistic procedure in connection with the Mother cult and Chapter Seven is the concluding chapter of this work detailing the distinctive features of the study. It not only sums up the discussions of the preceding chapters but also highlights the uniqueness of the Mātṛkā sculptures of our sub-continent.

I believe that my sincere attempt to deal with the present subject "**MATṚKA GODDESS VAIṢṆAVĪ**" will be of immense help to the scholars and students of history, archaeology, culture and of religion as it contains the evolution of Saktism, mythology and iconographic descriptions of the goddess Vaiṣṇavī. Lastly I crave the indulgence of the scholars for errors or omissions and commissions, which must have come in the course of my discussion.

ACKNOWLEDGEMENT

During the course of the last two decades in which the present work moved from conception to conclusion, many people have contributed to its accomplishment. It is my first and foremost duty to express a word of appreciation to those glorified personalities without whose able guidance the present work which is so vast and versatile, could not have been completed. I fail to select words to compliment this acknowledgement to Dr. Prof. Sadasiba Pradhan, Utkal University who has made the work colourful and alive by extending his help for planning, shaping and finishing it to acquire its present form and to enable it to fulfill a historical necessity.

I owe to my revered teachers and spiritual guide such as Dr. Maheswar Khadanga, Reader (retd) K.B.D.A.V. College, Nirakarpur, Late Pandit Sri Balabhabra Mahapatra, Sanskrit teacher, Late Pandit Samanta Vasudeva Mahapatra, Kulacharya, Late Sri Viswanath Ratha, Head Master (retd) and Swami Yogeswaranda Giri, Kriya Yogi, Karar Ashram, Puri without whose blessings and goodwill this task would not have been a successful one. Furthermore, I am very much grateful to late Dr. K.S. Behera, Senior Professor of History and late Dr. U.N. Dhal, Reader in Sanskrit, Dr. A.N. Parida, Reader in History, Utkal University who have helped me a lot for the completion of the present treatise.

I am obliged to the H.O.D Professor Dr. Ashok Kumar Pattanaik, Dr. Sanjay Acharya, Reader and Dr. Jayanti Dora,

Reader along with the faculty members of the Department of History and the Department of Ancient Indian History, Culture and Archeology, Utkal University for their suggestions and ungrudging help.

The Chief Librarian and the staff of the Parija Library, Utkal University Bhubaneswar; the staff members of the H.K. Mahatab, State Library, Bhubaneswar; Library, P.G. Department of History, Utkal University, Library, P.G. Department of Ancient Indian History, Culture and Archaeology, Vani Vihar, Utkal University; the Orissa State Museum, Bhubaneswar; the Archaeological Survey of India, Bhubaneswar Circle; the Department of State Archaeology, Bhubaneswar, have been greatly helpful to me in providing access to all requisite data, information and records I needed. I am extremely grateful to the authorities of all these institutions. Moreover, I am extremely grateful to the Superintendent Orissa State Museum, Superintendent State Archives Bhubaneswar for library facilities.

During the course of collection of valuable materials such as photographs, palm leaf manuscripts and other relevant information I met several resourceful persons. The number is so large that it is difficult to name them all. But I am extremely grateful to them and especially I offer my thanks to Dr. B.K. Rath, Ex-Superintendent, Department of State Archaeology, Dr. C.B. Patel, Superintendent, State Museum Bhubaneswar, Dr. H.C Das, Superintendent (Retd) Orissa State Museum, Bhubaneswar who have helped me immensely.

I acknowledge my indebtedness to the writers whose books I have consulted and from which I have taken not only materials but also drawn illustrations. The first and foremost is the book *Sakti Cult in Orissa* by Francesco Brighenti. The second major book is the *Archaeological Remains at Bhubaneswar* authored by Dr. Krishna Chandra Panigrahi. The third major book is the *Temples of Orissa* by Prof. Karuna Sagara Behera. The fourth major work is the *Hindu Goddesses* by David Kinsley and the fifth major work is the *Tantra and Śakta Art of Orissa* authored by Prof. Donaldson.

I render due reverence to my parents, elderly persons and accord my special thanks to my family members, wife and colleagues for their wise counsel, constant support and encouragement in many ways through the years for the completion of the present work.

I extend my sincere thanks to Sri Mrutyunjay Palai, Software Developer for completing the computer typing of the manuscript. I am also thankful to the present publisher who has extended his help for completion of the book in time.

Lastly, with steadfastness of devotion I bow my head at the lotus-feet of the Divine Mother without whose benign grace and blessings the present work would not have been accomplished.

Dr. Sanjaya Kumar Mahapatra

LIST OF TABLES

LIST OF MAPS/CHARTS

LIST OF PLATES

ABBREVIATIONS

A.A	Artibus Asiatique
A.D.	Anno Domini
A.P	Andhra Pradesh
A.R.	Asiatic Research
A.S.B.	Asiatic Society of Bengal
A.S.I.	Archeological Survey of India
AGP	Agni Purāṇa
ASIAR	Archaeological Survey of India Annual Report
BHVP	Bhavishya Purāṇa
Cf.	Compare (confer)
Ch.	Chapter
DBP	Devī Bhāgavata Purāṇa
DM	Devī Mahātmya
DP	Devī Purāṇa
e.g.	Example gratia
E.I.	Epigraphica India
Ed.	Edited By
Eds.	Editors
Fig.	Figure
Fn.	Footnotes

i.e.	That is
I.H.Q.	Indian Historical Quarterly
Ibid	in the same place (ibidem)
J.A.H.R.S	Journal of the Andhra Historical Research Society
J.A.S.B.	Journal of the Asiatic Society of Bengal
J.B.O.R.S	Journal of Bihar and Orissa Research Society
J.I.H	Journal of Indian History
KLP	Kālikā Purāṇa
M.P.	Madhya Pradesh
MASI	Memoir of Archaeological Survey of India
Mbh	Mahābhārata
MP	Mārkaṇḍeya Purāṇa
MTSP	Matsya Purāṇa
N.A.H.O.	New Aspects on History of Orissa
No.	Number
O.H.R.J.	Orissa Historical Research Journal, Bhubaneswar
O.U.P.	Oxford University Press
Op. cit.	The work cited (opere citato)
P.	Page
P.I.H.C.	Proceeding of Indian History Congress.
pp.	Pages
RV	RigVeda
SKP	Skanda Purāṇa
SP	Śiva Purāṇa
Tr	Translated by
VDP	Viṣṇudharmōttara Purāṇa
Viz.	Namely
Vol.	Volume
VP	Vāmana Purāṇa
VRP	Varāha Purāṇa

Contents

1

INTRODUCTION

Sṛṣṭi-sthiti-vināśānāṁ śaktibhūte sanātanī
guṇāśraye guṇamaye Nārāyaṇī namostute
(*Devī-Mahātmya,* ch.XI.11)

Śakti, the cradle of the phenomenal existence of beings, plays a vital role not only in India but also in the whole world. She is the source of cosmic evolution and the controller of all forces and potentialities of nature. She is the immediate cause of the perceptible world and all the beings are in her domain. As such, to know her in the entirety is to know her reality. To add more, Saktism is the worship of Śakti or the female principle, the primary factor in the creation, sustenance and dissolution of the universe. The term Śakti represents divinity in general and stands for the energizing power of some divinity in particular[1]. Being feminine in gender she has long been associated with the various male deities as their energy but in Saktism the energy of each God becomes personified as his consort, and thus, if a god is separated from his consort or Śakti, he is powerless and inert. To justify this statement, Śankarāchārya, the propounder of monistic theory, in the Saundaryalaharī[2] has eulogised the greatness of Śakti in the following manner:

Śivaḥ śaktyā yukto yadi bhavati śaktaḥ prabhavituṁ
na ced evaṁ devo na khalu kuśalaḥ spanditumapi;
ata stvāṁ ārādhyāṁ Hari-Hara-Viriñcādibhir api
praṇantuṁ stotuṁ vā katham akṛta-puṇyaḥ prabhavati

(*Saundaryalaharī, sloka* I)

Concept of Śakti

The word Śakti is derived from the root 'Śak' meaning the capacity to have power and to perform[3]. It indicates both capacity and activity. It may also be applied to any form of action like seeing, hearing, smelling etc. These are all powers of activity which are ultimately reducible to the primordial energy (*Ādyā*-Śaktī) from where every other form of power proceeds[4]. Further, Śakti may be conceived to be the personification of universal energy in abstract. She resides in the macrocosm and microcosm. While all the forms of activity in the perceptible world are the manifestation of the macrocosmic forms of Śakti, in the microcosmic form she resides dormant in the human body at thebottom of the spinal column (*mulādhāra chakra*). The ultimate aim of Yoga *śāstras* is to arouse it and carry it to the cerebrum (*sahasrāra chakra*) for attainment of *samādhi*, the ever blissful state.

It is said that since the dawn of civilization when the primitive man lived in a matriarchal society the worship of the divine mother came into practice. Later on as civilization progressed the matriarchal pattern gradually faded away and the father became the head of the family unit. Consequently there was a change in the concept of God and the fatherhood of God was established. But simultaneously Mother Worship persisted along with the male-divinity since this concept was psychologically more appealing to the devotee. The conception of God as Mother is natural. She is *prakṛti*, goddess of Earth and Mother Supreme. She creates and devours the world in her benevolent and malevolent forms respectively. It is said in *Devī-Bhāgavata*[5], "There is only one reality and that is the Brahman, the Brahman and I am the same. I am neither male nor female. I am the power behind everything". *Devī-Mahātmya* says that she reveals herself in the form of consciousness in this world. She remains for ever while even Brahmā, Viṣṇu and Iśvara are subject to dissolution. She has no beginning and end. The power of her will or desire creates rules and destroys the world with its movable and immovable beings. Though she is formless she incarnates herself invarious forms to protect the world.

This aspect of Śakti is also eulogized by the Sankhya and Vedanta. The idea of the Sankhya that the *puruṣa* is by nature inactive and *prakṛti* active in the proximity of *puruṣa* and similarly the concept of Advaita Vedanta that Brāhma becomes the creator only when associated with *māyā,* the eternal power (*nityā* Śakti) really emphasized the goddess in her energetic as well as illusory aspects[6]. This *māya* is none other than *prakṛti* while the *māyin* is *puruṣa.* Alternatively in the theistic sectarian concept they become Śakti and Śiva. Moreover, in the fifth chapter of *Devī-Mahātmya*[7] it has been described that Śakti is embodiment of various virtues and abstract qualities such as *chetanā (*consciousness*)*, *buddhi* (intelligence), *nidrā* (sleep), *kṣudhā* (hunger), *chāyā* (shadow), *tṛṣnā* (thirst), *kṣānti* (patience), *śānti* (peace), *śraddhā* (faith), *smṛti* (memory) and *dayā* (compassion) etc. All these are metaphysical exposition and manifold manifestations of the one Energy (śakti). This concept of the *Devī-Mahātmya* greatly enhanced the greatness of the Mother Goddess and established her superiority over other gods and goddesses. However, this Śakti whose one of the manifestations is the mother goddess is generally *nigūḍha* or hidden[8]. Even the gods do not know her, for not infrequently they are puffed up with arrogance and conceit[9]. Besides, it is also delineated in the scriptures that the association of Śakti and Śiva is at the root of material and spiritual progress of mankind[10]. Men in all ages have realized the manifestation of Śiva through her in contemplation, and this has been possible only through worship.

Genesis of Śakti Cult

The various views regarding the genesis of the concept of Śakti and her cult are as follows:-

1. According to some the fertility theory in the Hindu conception of the earth as Mother[11] and its intimate

association with agriculture may be the origin of the Śakti cult.

2. Friedrich Heiler has opined that the conception of God as mother is as natural and ultimate as the concept of Him as father[12]. And it is just possible that the Indian concept of the Śakti cult is nothing but a part of the widespread worship of a Mother Goddess. Payne[13], in his work 'The Śāktas' speaks of the possibility of certain contacts between Knossos and Egypt on the one hand and Per-Āryan Indian on the other as early as the 3rd millennium B.C. leading to the worship of Mother goddess. In this regard the history of India, Baluchistan, Iran, Mesopotamia, Asia minor, Egypt etc. bear testimony to the worship of Mother goddess in pre-historic times.

3. Mackenzie advocates an Asiatic origin. He says that during the Brahmanic age, the Bhāratas, the inhabitants of "Middle Kingdom" started worshipping Bhāratī, a goddess not unlike the mother goddesses of Egypt and early Europe. This goddess became associated with 'Sarasvatī' and was ultimately recognized as the wife of Brahmā, the Supreme God. When Buddhism declined and Śiva became the most popular deity, this goddess worship was transformed to his consort and was organized into a separate sect[14].

4. Starbruck in his book Encyclopaedia of Religion and Ethics has mentioned that when the Āryan invaders settled in India and led a peaceful agricultural life, the worship of female deities rose to a position of supreme importance and among these were Durgā, the eternity, Sarasvatī, supreme wisdom and śakti, mother of all phenomena.

5. V.A. Smith[15] has held that the migrations of the nomads of the central Asian steppes, which culminated in the Kushāṇa or Indo-Scythian conquest in Northern India, must have caused this change in Hinduism.
6. Slater in the Oxford history of India has mentioned that the cult of Mothergoddess must have arisen first among the matriarchal tribes.
7. John Marshall[16] observes that the cult of mother goddess must have originated in Anatholia (probably in Phrygia) and from there must have spread throughout western Asia.

Saktism in Different Periods

The cult of Śakti has a profound influence on Indian thought, theology and religion since time immemorial. It was wide-spread in the past and has continued to the present day. For the sake of convenience, the history of Śakti cult may be classified into three periods.

1. Ancient or Pre-Buddhist, beginning with the pre-historic times.
2. Mediaeval or Post-Buddhist, rather Post-Christian up to the 12th century A.D.
3. Modern, from the 13th century onwards.

No independent work on the Śakti cult in the ancient period is available while the mediaeval was the most creative period in the history of the Śakti literature. Most of the standard works including *Purāṇas*, *Upapurāṇs* and original *Āgamas* (Tantras) were written in this period. Modern period too has been productive, but with a few brilliant exceptions most of the works produced in this period are of a secondary character.

Saktism in the Indus Valley Period

The beginning of the worship of Śakti goes back in India as in many other countries of the ancient world to a very remote past[17]. Sir John Marshall has compared a large number of female figurines of terracotta found both at Mohenjodāro and Harappā, with kindred examples from the neighboring country of Baluchistan. The figurines are generally portrayed in the form of standing and almost nude females, wearing a band of girdle about their loins with an elaborate, more or less crescent shaped head dress, occasionally with ornamented cheeks and a long necklace, and wearing ear-armaments which take the form of shell-like cups suspended by hands on either side of the head[18]. Large numbers of terracotta figures, very probably representing this goddess have been found in course of excavations from various sites of the Indus valley. The early settlers of this valley appear also to have worshipped the goddess in her aniconic form. Many ringstones, discovered at the sites can justifiably be described as cult-objects symbolising the mother aspect of the goddess[19]. These must be studied along with not only the much decorated types of ring stones of the Maurya period found in many north Indian sites like Taxila, Kośām, Rājghāt and Patna, but also phallic objects symbolizing the father god of the Indus Valley people, conveniently described by Marshall as Proto shrines. The ornamented ringstones of the historic period no doubt represent some variety, but their general character shows that they were cult objects comparable with the ring stones of the Indus Valley on the one hand and the *cakras* and the *yantras* of the later Śāktas on the other[20].

A seal unearthed at Harappā shows a nude female figure, upside down with legs wide apart, and with a plant issuing from her womb. Her arms are shown in the same position in which those of the Proto-Śiva on the Mohenjodāro seal amulet are depicted. Marshall has rightly compared this striking representation of the nude female figure with a plant issuing from her womb, with the almost similar example of early Gupta terracotta sealing showing a female figure with her legs in much the same position but with a lotus emerging from her neck instead of from her womb[21]. This idea of vegetation emerging from some part of the body of a female form can at once remind us of the *Devī-Mahātmya* concept of the Śākambarī aspect of the goddess. Thus, in the opinion of John Marshall, Śakti worship originated in India out of the cult of the mother goddess, and it was closely connected with the cult of Śiva. Śakti and Śiva are integrally linked[22] in Indian imagination, as the creative principle (power) and the creator, with a colourful family representing the collective organism of life[23].

The pre-Vedic archaeological data discussed above throws much light on the early stages of the cult long before it was fully developed into the Śakti worship of the Epic and the Puranic age. It seems that ancient people living in the primitive matriarchal society had a veneration and love for the mother, which culminated in mother worship.

Concept of Śakti in the Vedas

The concept of Śakti was there in the minds of Vedic seers (though the term Śakti is not found in Vedic texts), is proved by the fact that a number of goddesses are mentioned in different capacities. The ancient Ṛṣis assigned importance to such goddesses as Aditi, the Divine Mother, Uṣās, the goddess of dawn; Pṛthivī, the mother of Earth; and lastly Vāc, the goddess of speech. These three distinguishable types of Mother Goddesses in the Ṛgveda viz[24].

1. The type of mother goddess for giving kindness and gentleness is represented by Aditi.
2. The type of virgin mother goddess for martial spirit and beauty is represented by Uṣās.

3. The type of mother goddess who is regarded as a tutelary or special guardian deity of people is represented by Sarasvatī.

Moreover, Sarasvatī, primarily a river goddess (it was on the banks of this river that the distinctive traits of Vedic culture were formulated), Rātrī, the goddess personifying a star-lit night, Purandhi, Ilā and Dhīṣana, collectively, were also sung in some hymns of the Ṛgveda. But in the sublime conception of Vāc outlined in the *Devī-Sūkta* (R.V., X.1[25]) is to be found one of the greatest and at the same time simplest expositions of the concept of divine Energy or Śakti inherent in everything, in gods, men and animals, may in the Universe itself[25]. In a *Khila Rātrī-Śūkta*[26], Śakti is called the mother, the resort of all human beings. She is worshipped by the devotees for obtaining the fruits of their actions[27]. *Śrī-Śūkta* which forms an appendix as *Khila-Śūkta* of the Ṛgveda[28] praises the goddess Śrī, the goddess of wealth. Apart from the above cited goddesses,the other important goddesses of early Vedic period were Aditi, Uṣā, Sarasvatī, Vāc, Rātrī, Diti, Revatī, Indrāṇī, Varuṇānī and Agneyi etc. as mentioned by J.N.Banarjee[29]. It is to be noted that due to the impact of the non-Vedic people the goddesses like Ilā, Māhi, Puranidhī, Rākā, Kuhu, Sinivālī, Lakṣmī, Alakṣmī, Oṣadhi, Āpyā, Yosā, Gāndharvī etc.[30] also come into existence.

Now coming to the other Vedas which are generally taken to be later in point of time, we find the mention of the goddess Ambikā addressed as the sister of Rudra in the *Vājasaneyi Saṁhitā*[31], Ambikā is also mentioned in *Taittiriya Saṁhitā*. She is autumn in the *Taittiriya Brāhman*[32] and the *Satapatha Brāhman*[33]. Umā appears in the *Taittiriya Āraṇyaka* and in the same text Rudra is invoked as Umāpatī[34]. She is Umā Haimavatī in the *Kena Upaniṣad*[35]. *Śvetāśvetara Upaniṣad* refers to Māyā, the power of Brahman when Śiva is Māyin[36]. Bhadrakālī is mentioned in the *Sānkhyāyana Śrauta Śūtra* as well as in the *Gṛhya Śūtra*. In the *Bodhāyan Gṛhya Śūtra* and *Manu Saṁhitā*, Durgā and Jyeṣṭhā are mentioned and offering to them are prescribed[37]. Kālī, Karāli, Manojavā, Sulohitā, Viśva Rūpā, Sudhumravarṇā and Sphuliṅginī are the names of Agni's seven flames found in *Muṇḍaka Upaniṣad.* The names of Durgī, Vairochanī, Kātyāyanī and Kanyā Kumārī occur in the *Taittiriya Āraṇyaka*[38]. Besides, the various names of the mother goddess are also found in the *Tripurā Upaniṣad, Tripurā Tāpini Upaniṣad, Bhavānī Upaniṣad, Saubhagyā Lakṣmī Upaniṣad, Sitopaniṣad* and *Atharavaśīrsopaniṣad* etc. These Śākta *Upaniṣads* which can undoubtedly be said to belong to the later epochs in Indian History[39] which contain reference and glorification of the Śakti cult.

Concept of Śakti in the Epics and Purāṇas

In the age of Epics, Śakti is depicted in a very high position. She is called Devī and is respected by all[40]. In the Rāmāyaṇa she is always considered the wife of Śiva. Her name Umā and Girijā were very popular. Even she was regarded as Rudrāṇī and Pārvatī[41]. There are other references in the Rāmāyaṇa which indicate that the worship of mother goddess was quite well known to the tradition though not mentioned in clear terms. In the fifth book there is a mention of a goddess named Surasā who is told to be the mother of Nāgas[42]. There is another goddess in the Rāmāyaṇa named Siṁhikā seen by Hanumān. We find a mention that Laṅkā, the capital city of Rāvaṇa's kingdom was protected by a demon goddess[43] named Lankinī. Sītā, the wife of Rāma is described as Kāla Rātrī, the terrible aspect of Śakti[44]. Even Sītā took the form of Kālī for the destruction of Rāvaṇa is found in the two later Rāmāyaṇas viz. *Adhyātma Rāmāyaṇa*[45] and *Abdhuta Rāmāyaṇa*. The following statements of other *Purāṇas* also support the prevalence of Śakti cult in the age of Rāmāyaṇa.

1. The Kurma Purāṇa[46] mentions the worship of Durgā by the king Janaka of Mithila.
2. Padma Purāṇa[47] states that the goddess was worshipped by a king named Sumada who fought with Śatrughna, the brother of Rāma.
3. Kaushalyā, the mother of Rāma is said to have worshipped Durgā, in Adhyātma Rāmāyaṇa[48].
4. Brahmavaivarta Purāṇa mentions that goddess Durgā was worshipped by Rāma and Parśurāma[49].
5. Rāmacharita Mānasa also describes the worship of Pārvatī by Sītā to get Rāma as her spouse.

Concept of Śakti in the Mahābhārata and Harivaṁśa Purāṇa

The cult of Śakti attained a great importance in the age of Mahābhārata. During the period of Mahābhārata many new names and aspects of the goddess were introduced. In the *Bhiṣma Parvaṁ* there is a prayer by Arjuna to Durgā in which he invokes and pays reverence to Siddhasenānī (leader of Siddhas), the noble, the dweller on Mandara, the Kumārī, Kālī, Kapālī, Kṛsnā-Piṅgalā, Bhadrakālī, Mahākālī, Caṇḍī, Chaṇḍā, Tāriṇī, Varavarṇinī, Kātyāyanī, Karālī, Vijayā, Jayā etc. In the *Virāta Parvaṁ* of the Mahābhārata, Yudhiṣṭhira, one of the five Pāṇḍavas invoked the goddess of power who would remove dangers which would occur to his devotees. She is represented in this chapter as the sister of Hari[50], born of Yaśodā and Nanda Gopa. She is praised as the feminine side of Kṛsna[51] and Kumārī or the maiden[52]. The two *Durgāstotras* in the Mahābhārata (IV.6 and VI.23) and the *Āryāstava* in its supplement (Harivaṁśa, III.3) outline the various constituent elements underlying the principal cult picture of the developed Śakti cult. The concept of the composite goddess contained in its various elements such as her 'mother' 'daughter' and 'sister' aspects, her Vedic Āryan element (cf. her appellations Āryā, Kauśikī, Kātyāyanī, i.e. 'the Āryan goddess', 'the goddess of the Kuśika and Kātyā sage clans') and last but not the least, the various non-Āryan strands in her character. The *Āryāstava*[53]says that she was well worshipped by the Śavaras, the Barbaras, and the Pulindas, and she is often described in other contexts as Aparṇā[54], Nagna Śavarī and Parṇa Śavarī. She is also commanded respect and adoration from the higher class including the nobles and kings (as she is worshipped by Yuddhiṣṭira, Arjuna, Pradyumna and *Aśvatthāmā*). In the *Vanaparva* of the Mahābhārata there is mention of various Devī *tirthas* (sacred places of Devī worship) viz. Śrī Parvata[55], Gaurī Śikhara, Śrī *tirtha*, Devī *tirtha* and Mātṛ *tirtha*[56] etc.

The above discussions give a clear picture about the prevalence of Śakti in the time of Rāmāyaṇa, Mahābhārata and *Harivaṁśa Purāṇa*.

Concept of Śakti in the Mārkaṇḍeya Purāṇa

The *Mārkaṇḍeya Purāṇa*, one of the oldest *Purāṇa*, was compiled and edited in its present form in the Gupta period[57]. There comes a complete book under the *Mārkaṇḍeya Purāṇa* consisting of 13 chapters named as *Durgā Saptaśatī* or *Devī-Mahātmya*. The *Devī-Mahātmya* is an elaboration of the concept of Devī of the Vedic doctrine[58], of an all powerful Goddess of supreme transcendence as propounded in the *Āmbhṛṇi Śūkta* and *Dākṣāyanī Śūkta*[59]. The *Saptaśatī* speaks of the goddess Caṇḍī, who represents a consolidated idea of different aspects of the divine truth as divine power. Here the mother goddess identified as Umā or Pārvatī is associated with the Himālayas[60]. In *Mārkaṇḍeya Purāṇa* the goddess Durgā is pure consciousness, (*Chiti*) power of Śiva and the *Māyā* of Viṣṇu (*viṣṇu māyeti śavditā*)[61]. She is *Prakṛti*, the primal rootevolvement[62]. She is also represented as hunger, thirst, sleep, memory etc. She exists in them as her reflections (*Chāyā rūpeṇa saṁsthitā*)[63]. She is also regarded as Mahāvidyā, Mahāmāyā, Mahāsurī and Mahāmohā[64]. In her Mahākālī-Mahālakṣmī-Mahāsarsvatī aspects, she is depicted in killing the demons like Madhukaiṭava, Mahiṣāsura and Śumbha-Niśumbha as delineated in the *Prathama*, *Madhyama* and *Uttama Charita* of the *Devī-Mahātmya.* In *Devī Bhāgavat Purāṇa* Śakti is addressed as *Brahamavidyā* and *Sarvachaitanyarūpā*[65]. Another passage describes Devī as Vaiṣṇavī and Śankarī[66]. She is also Bhuvaneśvarī, the great lady of the world[67]. Besides, *Vāyu Purāṇa*, *Agni Purāṇa*, *Matsya Purāṇa*, *Brahma Vaivarta Purāṇa*, *Vāmana Purāṇa* and *Bhaviṣya Purāṇa* also contain the descriptions about Śakti-worship.

It is apparent that all the *Purāṇas* are full of her majestic grace and superiority over all other gods. Sometimes we find the *Purāṇas* eulogising her as Brahman, while others specifically say that she is the power of Śiva, the Śaktīmān.

Concept of Śakti in other Texts

In the mediaeval period Tāntricism intermingled with Brāhmanical Hinduism, Mahāyānism and with Vajrayāna forms of Buddhism attained full development in India (especially predominant in eastern part). Śakti worship was also popular in many places of the extreme south-west of India, and tradition says that Śankarāchārya, the greatest exponent of Advaitavāda, was an ardent devotee of the goddess. He is said to have composed in her honour the famous Tāntric text Saundaryalaharī and an authoritative commentary on the *Lalitā Sahasranāma*[68] (one thousand names of Lalitā). Further, *Vāmakeśvaratantra* says that creation, preservation and destruction are maintained by the Śrichakra only. The sound form of the goddess is Śrīvidyā mantra and her line form (*yantra*) is Śrīchakra. Śrīchakra is the combination of Śiva and Śakti. In *Brahma Yāmala Tantra*, while explaining the greatness of Śakti, Brahmā said to Vasiṣṭha, "She is supreme Śakti. She protects the beings of the worlds. Her action is spread throughout the moving and motionless objects. So worship her[69]. In the *Kulacūḍāmaṇinigama*, the Bhairavī addressing Bhairava says "Thou art in every place and I am in every place. Thou art in all and I am in all". However, *Mahānirvāṇa Tantra*[70] describes her as the *Prāṇaśakti* (life force) of Paramātmā, the Supreme Soul. As such, the creative world sows its seeds in her womb for procreation. Besides, the most extensive exposition of the worship of Śakti is found in the Tantras in the form of Daśa-Mahāvidyās, the usual classification of the goddess.

Śrī Rāmakrishna Paramahaṁsa, an elevated saint of India has expounded a simple theory of Saktism in the 18th century. He realised all the gods and goddesses in the form of Kālī. His relationship with Kālī was that of a mother and child. He believed that various images of the goddess are the mediums to understand the formula of all pervading power[71]. So to him Brahman and Kālī are the same. Later in the 20th century Śrī Aurobinda (The Mother, p.36 ff.) interpreted the doctrine of Śakti in a new light. According to him the Śakti is the driving force of all evolutions. The *Sādhaka* should surrender himself without any reservation to the will of the Mother. Again he emphasized on the four great aspects of the Divine Mother along with her leading powers and personalities in her dealing with the terrestrial play. The names of four personalities are Māheśvarī, Mahākālī, Mahālakṣmī and Mahāsarasvatī. To add more, from the middle of the 20th century A.D the Śakti cult began to contribute to the growth of Indian Nationalism. The concept of the country in the form of Divine Mother became a strong basis of Indian freedom movement. In the words of Śrī Aurobinda "Mother India is not a piece of earth, she is power, a god head, for all nations have such a Devī supporting their separate existence and keeping it in being". The real instigator of Mother Consciousness in national life was Bankimchandra. He identified the mother India with female divinity in his text "*Vandemātaraṁ*". Vivekānanda also regarded the country as the living image of the Divine Mother.

From the above discussion it is quite obvious that the cult of Śakti is primitive as well as pre-historic and may have started among the primitive tribes, but on the grounds of Vedic references to Saktism, we have to conclude that it was also Vedic in the sense that the followers of Vedic religion practised it. Changing and developing from time to time, the concept of Saktism forms the guiding principle of the agriculturists to that of the movement of national awakening. Thus, we have the continuous development of the Saktism starting from the pre-historic times to the present day for the betterment of the society and spiritual upliftment of the mankind as a whole.

Saktism in Orissa

Śakti cult played an important role in the socio-religious life of the Orissan people. The archeological as well as literary sources prove the prevalence of Śakti cult in Orissa to an early age. Both in paintings and engravings of Orissan rock art several instances of bisected triangles resembling female genital have been encountered[72]. Repeated occurrences of such symbols in the different rock shelters amply suggest the popularity of the primordial mother cult or the cult of fecundity during the prehistoric period. Discovery of perforated stones in rock shelters, the other objects related to Saktism from Neolithic and Chalcolithic sites and the Yoni stone found from the district of Kalahandi and Nuāpaḍā region have often proved the beginning of Śakti cult in Orissa to a hoary past. Besides, one of the earliest references appears in the line six of Rock Edict XIII of Aśok which alludes to the mother-worship by the Atavīkas who lived in the forest regions of Kaliṅga[73]. The writings of Sāralā Dās, celebrated author of Oriya literature also illustrates this point. This greate poet has written a special version of the Mahābhārata in the 15th century A.D. which supports the prevalence and popularity of Saktism in Orissa. Every today, as pointed out by B.C Pradhan, the Divine Mother, usually in the form of a post or a pillar, is worshipped in virtually every forest (*atavī*) region in Orissa while the concept of Vana Durgā became especially popular in the medieval period[74]. Non-Āryan tribes like Śavaras and the Pulindas who were the inhabitants of the forest area of Mahendragiri Mountain, as indicated in the early Orissan inscriptions[75] as well as in the Sanskrit works such as Kathāsaritsāgara[76], were great devotees of the Divine Mother. Like the phallus-worship resembling Lord Śiva, the worship of Śakti in the form of a log of wood, a post, or a stone pillar (*stambha*) most likely evolved from primitive tree worship. In Orissa this form of the Divine Mother is often designated as Stambheśvarī (Khambheśvari), or as Kandhuṇidevī i.e. the deity of the aboriginal khonds[77].

The earliest epigraphic reference to the tribal goddess in Orissa appears in the Bhadrak inscription of Mahārājā Suraśarmā, dated on Palaeological ground to the 3rd century A.D., where the goddess Parṇṇadevatī (goddess of leaves or forest) received donations of garments, gold and a pedestal from a lady named Raṅghāli[78]. The tradition of worshipping the goddess of leave under the name Patarasuṇī is still prevalent in the rural areas of Orissa[79]. By the 4th century A.D. due to the influence of south Indian campaign of Samudragupta[80], Brāhmanical form of Hinduism percolated into the tribal hinter lands of ancient Kośala and Kaliṅga leading to the transformation of the tribal Stambha/Khamba or the pillar to Stambheśvarī or Khambheśvari. Moreover, the copper plate of Terāsingā refers to Bhagavatī Stambheśvarī as the tutelary deity of Mahārajā Tuṣṭikara, whose mother Śrī Śobhinī Kaustubheśvarī was an ardent devotee of Stambheśvarī. The charter was issued at a place named Parvatadvāra (gateway to mountains)[81]. The Stambheśvarī cult still survives at the village level in western Orissa and temples are also erected in the honour of Stambheśvarī at Sonepur and at Aska.

In addition to the ethnographic and epigraphic records, the sacred religious texts such as *Mahābhārata*, *Vāyu Purāṇa*, *Brahma Purāṇa*, *Kapila Saṁhitā*, *Caṇḍī Purāṇa*, *Kubjikā Tantra*, *Virajā-Kṣetra Mahātmya*, *Baṭa Abakāsa* etc. also refer to the prevalence of Śakti cult in Orissa. Starting from the Śailodbhavas down to the rule of the Gajapati kings Saktism in one form or the other has crept into the socio-religious beliefs of the Orissan people.

Saktism in Gupta Period

Śakti cult in the form of female divinity especially the deity of Virajā at Jājpur made its appearance in Orissa during the Gupta period. The image is assigned to pre-Gupta period by R.P.Chanda[82] and Gupta period by K.C. Panigrahi[83]. The two armed deity Virajā represents the earliest form of Śakti in Orissa. During the post-Gupta period the cult of Stambeśvarī, the other important goddess cult of Orissa was sanskritised and became the family deity of the Sulki dynasty of Kodālaka Maṇḍala (A.D.600-900)[84], as evidenced from the epigraphic records. In the same period the rulers of Kaṅgoda kingdom, Śailodbhavas were the devout worshippers of Śiva along with Pārvatī. For the first time in the history of Orissan inscriptions we find an invocatory verse pertaining to the divine couple of Śambhu (Śiva) and Pārvatī (Śakti) in the preamble of the undated Buguḍā charter[85] of Mādhavarāja II of the Śailodbhava dynasty. Another important epigraphical record of Śailodbhavas which sheds light on the Śākta *pīṭha* of Orissa is the Bāṇapur copper plate grant of Dharmarāja Śrīmānabhita making endowments for the presiding deity Bhagavatī. Further, Śākta images were also carved on the outer walls of some Śaivite temples of Bhubaneswar due to the patronage of Śailodbhavas which clearly indicate the syncretic cult of *Śākta-pāśupata*[86] during 6th-7th century A.D. Apart from these, the Śākta shrines of Tārā-Tāriṇī of Puruṣottamapur and Śikharacaṇḍī of Patiā also reveal the worship of mother goddess during the regime of Śailodbhava dynasty.

Saktism in Bhauma-Kara Period

The entire history of the Bhauma-kara dynasty is quite emblematic of the modalities of expansion of Saktism in Orissa in a period marked for the integration of goddess-cult with Śaivism and Mahāyāna Buddhism on the common religious background formed by *Tāntric* ideals and practices then in ascent in the Oriya society[87]. Although there was not a single Bhauma ruler who embraced Saktism as an independent faith yet the Dhenkanal copper plate grant[88] of Tribhuvana Mahādevī provides references to two female deities Kātyāyanī and Siddha Gaurī. The inscription[89] on an image of Cāmuṇḍā at Jājapur also reveals that Vātsadevī, a queen of the Bhauma period patronized this cult of Saptamātṛkās particularly that of Cāmuṇḍā. Besides, some monumental and sculptural representations of the Bhauma period also throw focus on the prevalence of Śakti cult in Orissa. The Śākta shrines of Vaitāl, Mohinī and Uttareśvara of Bhubaneswar, the Khiching temple of Mayurbhanja and Śākta images of Prachi Valley still remind us about the spread of Saktism in Orissa during the Bhauma-kara rule. Moreover, the tribal pillar goddess Stambheśvarī was patronised by the Bhauma-karas and Bhañjas of Khiñjalimaṇḍala as evidenced from the copper plate grants[90] of these two dynasties. Thus, we can conclude that the religious policy during the Bhauma-kara rule aimed at conciliating *Tāntric* Buddhism, the dynasty's original faith, with Saktism and Śaivism, the dominant faiths among the Oriyas at the time when the Bhaumas became the sovereigns of the country[91].

Saktism in Somavaṁśī Period

The Somavaṁśī Kings, though Śaivas by faith, patronised Śakti in a large scale during the early years of their rule. It is striking to note that the Somavaṁśīs have saluted Bhagavatī Pañcāmbarī as the presiding deity of Suvarṇapura, their first capital in Kosala as it is evidenced from the Marañjamura charter[92]. In the Brahmeśvara temple inscription at Bhubaneswar, Somavaṁśī ruler Yayati II is recorded as Caṇḍīhara since he was an ardent devotee of both Caṇḍī (Śakti) and Hara (Śiva)[93].

The dominant trend in the Somavaṁśī period was directed in softening or eliminating the most awful and gruesome aspects of Śakti-worship which had its popularity in Orissa during the Bhauma-kara period. The best instance of this new trend was that all the Śākta shrines erected by Somavaṁśīs at Bhubaneswar were presided over by the goddesses in pacific form. The Khākharā temple dedicated to the goddess Gaurī in the Kedāra-Gaurī temple compound (10th century A.D.)[94] as well as two other such shrines respectively dedicated to the goddess Gopālinī and Sāvitrī in the Liṅgarāja complex (12th century A.D)[95] testify, by virtue of the non-fearful aspect of their own presiding deities, to the more moderate course imparted to the Śakti cult at Bhubaneswar by the Somavaṁśī rulers.

It is noteworthy to mention that the benevolent, motherly and nurturing aspect of the Matṛkās associating each of these deities with a baby placed on their lap developed during the period of Somavaṁśīs. The earlier Matṛkā images of Orissa do not hold babies in their arms while, on the other hand, the baby-in-lap motif is present in the set of Matṛkās found at Rāṇīpur-Jhariāl[96] and Belakhandi in the Bolangir-Kalahandi regions, two sites of Somavaṁśī art assigned to the 9th-10th centuries A.D.. The Mātṛkās of Mukteśvara temple at Bhubaneswar, Daśāśvamedhaghāṭ at Jājapur, Mārkaṇḍeśvara at Puri and the collapsed Mātṛkā temple at Sāthalapur in Cuttack district are assignable to the initial part of the Somavaṁśī rule over coastal Orissa[97].

The incorporation of the folk goddess Maṅgalā into the Brāhmanical Śākta pantheon of Orissa was also another achievement of the Somavaṁśī dynasty. It appears that the Somavaṁśī rulers were responsible for the Sanskritisation of the popular semi-tribal cult of Maṅgalā, which in subsequent epochs would have formed a sort of religious bridge uniting Orissan Saktism to Vaiṣṇavīsm[98].

To conclude the sketch of the development of Śakti cult in Orissa during the Somavaṁśī period, mention is here to be made of the triumph, occurred in that epoch, of the female body in the field of sculptural art and highlighting the female beauty, grace, warmth and sensuousness inherent in the moderate *kaula* doctrines fostered by the Somavaṁśī monarchs.

Saktism in Gaṅga Period

The Gaṅga monarchs of Orissa seemingly endeavoured to eliminate Saktism as an independent form of religion and to make it subservient to the major male-oriented Hindu cults which were in their turn made subservient to the national cult of Jagannāth. In support of this view a tradition recorded in the Mādalā Pañji, the chronicle of the temple of Jagannāth at Puri, states that Coḍagaṅga banished all goddesses from Orissa. Another tradition mentioned in a copy of the same chronicle recovered from Berhampur indicates that Coḍagaṅga was antagonistic to all the Śākta images except a few like Virajā at Jājpur, this goddess being considered to be a part of *pañcadevatā-upāsanā* fostered by the Gaṅgas themselves[99]. The prevalent trend of Devī worship during the Imperial Gaṅga period was to provide all the male divinities with the female consorts, whose cult icons were enshrined in the minor temples built in the compound of each great Orissan temple dedicated to Hindu God[100]. Most probably, the Gaṅgas intended in this way to show the people their religious catholicity making a room for the Śakti cult in the premises of the male divinities and at the same time, to deny the role of the Devī as an independent cult heroine.

The Gaṅgas earned the fame for building a shrine for the goddess Pārvatī, second in magnitude only to the main temple itself, in the Liṅgarāja temple complex at Bhubaneswar. The temple was dedicated to Pārvatī in her form as Arnnapūrnā (the giver of food and plenty or the goddess of nourishment, the vegetable-bestowing and food giving aspect of the Devī representing the later power of given plentiful crops). At the holy place of Puri, whose presiding deity was Jagannāth, the emperor Coḍagaṅga erected a subsidiary shrine for the worship of Lakṣmī, the goddess of wealth considering her as the consort of that great god[101]. This shrine, which in point of importance is only next to the main temple, later on exceeded in popularity as the Pīṭheśvarī Vimalā, the Śākta *Tāntric* goddess.

The Śākta *Tāntric* influence is also noticed in the daily rituals of Jagannāth temple. For instance, the cult image of Jagannāth is placed on a *Śrīcakra-yantra* and is worshipped in the *bīja-mantra klīm* (termed as *kāma-bīja*, the seed of desire) which represents the procreative power of the universal Śakti. Moreover, the Saudarsiṇī *Vāmadeva Saṁhitā*, a *Tāntric* text, states that Jagannāth is the very self of Dakṣiṇa Kālīkā[102].

The Śākta devotees of Orissa recognise Puri as one of the traditional Śākta *pīṭhas* where Vimalā is regarded as Bhairavī and Jagannāth, merely as her Bhairava[103]. (*Vimalā Yatra Bhairavī Jagannāthastu Bhairavaḥ*). Even the deity Subhadrā has been identified with Kātyāyanī in the *Puruṣottama Mahātmya* of the *Skanda Purāṇa*[104]. At the *arka kṣetra* of Koṇārk, where the huge and magnificent Sūrya temple erected by the Gaṅga emperor Narasiṁha Deva (A.D.1238-64) stands in half-ruined conditions not far from the seashore, the female counterpart of the presiding God, (the sun) was Chāyā, whose collapsed shrine still exists to the south-west of the main temple. The Vaiṣṇava Trinity enshrined in the sanctum of the temple of Ananta-Vāsudeva at Bhubaneswar (AD1278), was formed by the cult icons of Kṛsna, Balarāma and Ekanaṁsā. Here Ekanaṁsā/Subhadrā conceived as the younger sister of Kṛsna and Balarāma as per the Mahābhārata and Harivaṁśa conform her iconography as Pārvatī which is smaller in size than those of the two male deities flanking her on both sides. Besides, an inscription of the Ananta-Vāsudeva temple states that Choḍagaṅga was not only a hero but an emperor also and performed the worship of the goddess after his victory over the hostile kings[105].

The brick temple of Motiā in the Prachi Valley, the Gaṅgeśvari temple of Bayālisbāṭi near Koṇārk are the Śākta shrines which bear the testimony to the prevalence of Śakti cult during the period of the Gaṅgas. The addition of Śaktis for the *dikpālas* and tutelary deities for the military establishments (goddesses of forts) strengthen further the concept of Saktism under the Gaṅga rule.

Saktism in Suryavaṁśī Period

The Suryavaṁśīs or the Gajapatis, who succeeded the Gaṅgas did not introduce any new feature into the ritualistic pattern of Saktism. Rather they adhered themselves to the Gaṅga tradition of religious tolerance and eclecticism. Although no Śākta temple of significance was erected in Orissa yet the emergence of the two Śākta centers such as Śyāmākālī near the old royal palace at Puri and Ugratārā at Bhusaṇḍapur in Khurda district are note worthy from the view point of the continuation and spread of Saktism during the rule of the Suryavaṁśī Gajapatis.

The cult of Lakṣmī which is essentially a house hold rural form of Śakti-worship, having little connection with the community worship in temples, however, gained a tremendous popularity in Orissa starting from the Suryavaṁśī period. The Oriya women were regarded responsible for the wealth and prosperity of their family members, for whose benefit they had to perform the daily religious rites properly with a special accent on the propitiation of the goddess Lakṣmī. The ideal of womanliness typical of a patriarchal society was thus expressed at best in the cult of Lakṣmī[106].

The revival of Śākta literature during this period also indicates the eminence of Śakti worship in Orissa. The important Śākta literatures composed in this period were the *Mahālakṣmī Purāṇa* of Balarāma Dāsa, the *Caṇḍī Purāṇa* of Sāralā Dāsa, ŚaivaŚākta doctrines of Jagannāth Dāsa, Gitagovinda of Jayadeva etc. Gajapati Puruṣottama deva was a devotee of Durgā as evidenced from a copper plate inscription issued by him to Poṭeśvara Bhatta in 1471 A.D. He was also credited with the composition of two Śākta works written in praise of Durgā and Bhubaneswarī respectively[107].

The feudal rulers of the hinterlands of Orissa preferably used to worship as their tutelary deity a form of the great goddess, this being a very natural choice in a land where Śakti cult was the predominant form of religion. The tutelary deity gradually assumed the form of *Iṣṭadevatā* of the ruling family of Orissa during the medieval period. However, in the later medieval period some local goddesses of Orissa also rose to prominence as the tutelary deities of some feudatory families. The following examples may be taken into account to justify the above statement.

1. Kīchakeśvarī was the tutelary deity of the Bhañjas of the Khijingakoṭṭa[108] in the present Mayurbhanja district.
2. Tāriṇī of Ghaṭagaon[109] was the tutelary deity of the Bhañjas of Keonjhar.
3. Hiṅgulā of Gopālprasād was the tutelary deity of the Nala and Sulki rulers of Tālcher area of Dhenkanal district.
4. Maṇināga Devī[110] was the tutelary deity of royal family of Raṇpur in Nayagarh district.
5. Vyāghra Devī was the tutelary deity of the Bhañjas of Ghumsara at Kulāḍha in Ganjam district.
6. Bhairavī was the tutelary deity of the Rājās of Boudh.
7. Pāṭṇeśvarī was the tutelary deity of the Chauhan rulers of Pāṭṇāgarh in Bolangir district.
8. Samaleśvarī was the tutelary deity of the Chauhān[111] rulers in Sambalpur district.
9. Samaleśvarī enshrined at Suvarnapur was the tutelary deity of the Chauhan rulers of Suvarnapur.
10. Maṇikeśvarī at Bhawanipāṭaṇā[112] was the tutelary deity of the *Nāga* royal family of Kalahandi district.
11. Baruṇei and Aruṇei were the tutelary deities of the Bhoi dynasty of Khurda district etc.

With the increasing popularity of Vaiṣṇava cult, with that of Jagannāth eventually being elevated to the state religion, royal patronage of Saktism became absorbed by Vaiṣṇavīsm. Images of Devī were often housed in the sanctum with Mādhava while in the cult of Puruṣottam the deity was always worshipped together with the Śakti, the latter being transformed into Subhadrā in the cult of Jagannāth, which absorbed all of the religious cults into itself. Thus, prehistorical development of Śakti cult in Orissa was not one and the same in all the parts of the territory.

The Śākta Pīṭhas in Orissa

The descriptive myth of the Śākta *pīṭha*s is another expression of the Hindu intuition that the Indian sub-continent itself is a goddess. India is covered with prominent geographical features of the country. Mountains, hills, rivers, caves and other sites having some natural peculiarities are often affirmed to possess sacred power or to be places where one may make contact with the divine. These sites are usually called *tirthas*, where one may cross over from the realm of the profane to the sacred, from the human to the divine, from this world to another world. In many cases these sites are associated with deities who are well known in the Hindu tradition and who have an elaborate mythology[113].

The meaning of the word '*pīṭha'* is '*āsana'* or 'seat' (*Śavdakalpadruma*). The different *pīṭhas* in India supposed to be the dwelling places of the Devī (The mother goddess), that is why they are also called "*devīsthānas*". To a Śākta devotee the world *pīṭha* further bears a special significance. It includes such places where it is believed, the different parts of Satī's body fell after Viṣṇu cut into pieces[114]. Therefore, all the *pīṭhas* arc the *devīsthānas* but all the *devīsthānas* are not necessarily the *pīṭhas*. In this connection it may be noted that the places which are associated with the Mother goddess yet without holding Devī's physical parts are known as *upapīṭhas*. Some *devīsthānas* on the other hand are called *siddhapīṭhas* where at least one *sādhaka* must have attained realization or *siddhi*[115].

There are myths and legends in different *Purāṇas* and *Tantras* which attempt to explain the legend connected with Satī, the spouse of Śiva, on whose physical parts the *pīṭhas* have developed.

The legend of Dakṣa-Yajña as narrated in the Mahābhārata is of great importance in connection with the origin of Śākta *pīṭhas*. The *Harivaṁśa*, the *Kālīkā Purāṇa, Devī Bhāgavata, Śākta Upapurāṇas, Hevajra Tantra, Rudrayāmala Tantra, Kubjikā Tantra* etc. have coined several Śākta *pīṭhas* accelerating the cause of Saktism in the country. However the early *Tāntric* texts have mentioned about the four *pīṭhas* viz. 1.Jālandhara, 2.Uḍḍiyāna, 3.Pūrṇagiri and 4.Kāmarūpa. The *chatuspīṭha* conception may have been associated with the Sahajayāniya School of the Buddhists according to which one can rise to eternal bliss from sexual pleasure[116]. The *pīṭhas* were multiplied after the compilation of the *Pīṭhanirṇaya, Śivacharita, Kālīkā Purāṇa* and *Devī Bhāgavata* though the number of Śākta *pīṭhas* was limited to four as mentioned in the early *Tāntric* text "*Hevajra Tantra*" (7th century A.D.).

The ideology behind the *pīṭha* concept of holy centers devoted to Devī of her various names and the Bhairava forms stationed with her, evolves from the well-known mythology of Dakṣa's sacrifice and from the *Tāntric* texts. The number of *pīṭhas* each with a different manifestation, is increased to 108 in the *Matsya Purāṇa* (13.26-53), the *Skanda Purāṇa* (Revā-khaṇḍa,98.64-92), the *Padma Purāṇa* (17.184-211), *Devī Bhāgavata Purāṇa* (7.30.51-103), the *Prāṇaṭosiṇi Tantra* and one list in the (*Bṛhannīla Tantra patala V*). The number 108 has some importance to the sectarian worshippers who often attempt to endow their respective deities with 108 names[117]. However, the early *Tāntric* texts refer to four *pīṭhas* (*chatuspīṭhas*), such as Jālandhara, Uḍḍiyāna or Odiyāna, Pūrṇagiri or Pūrṇaśaila and Kāmarūpa. According to Tattvasāra there are five *pīṭhas* such as Uḍḍiyāṇa, Jālandara, Kāmarūpa, Pūrṇagriba and Śrihaṭṭa. *Hevajra Tantra* (composed before 693 A.D.) records four sacred *pīṭhas* such as Odra, Jālandhara, Pūrṇagiri and kāmarūpa. *Kubjikā Tantra*, *Jñanārṇava Tantra* and *Tantrasāra* enumerate fourtytwo, fifty and fiftyone Śākta *pīṭhas* respectively. The *Devī Bhāgavata* as well as *Kālikā Purāṇa* has furnished the list of *pīṭhas* which vary in number with different nomenclature.

Orissa was a land of primary importance in the *Tāntric* world. Out of four *pīṭhas* described in the early *Tāntric* texts, one of them namely Oḍḍiyāna may convincingly be located in Orissa. Although the scholars differ in their opinion regarding the location of this *pīṭha* but it can undoubtedly be identified with Orissa on the basis of the copper plate grant of Janmejaya I and the inscriptions of south India which refer Orissa as Odra or Oḍḍiyāna[118]. Another inscription of Sāluva Narasiṁha[119] Uḍḍiyāna Gālabi finds mention which supports the view that Oddiyāna is no other than Orissa. The term *pīṭha* is a conventional name for the territory of Orissa as it is evidenced from the *Rudrayāmala* and *Jñānārṇava Tantra*. For example, in *Rudrayāmala* the name of the *pīṭha* is Kaliṅga and in *Jñānārṇava* the name of the *pīṭha* is Uḍḍissā[120]. Even in the *Śivacarita*, Utkal is regarded as a *Mahāpīṭha*. Keeping in view the Śākta *pīṭha* legends of Orissa it can be said that a large number of Śākta centers have developed in the ancient and medieval periods either under the patronage of the royal dynasties or by the people of the respective religions about which references are found in the *Kapila Saṁhitā*, the *Ekāmra Purāṇa*, the *Ekāmra Chandrikā* and in the *Svarṇādrimahodaya*[121]. Among the described Śākta *pīṭhas*, there are eight prominent Śākta centers which are regarded as *Aṣṭa-Kīlā* or *Aṣṭa-Caṇḍī pīṭhas* of Orissa as mentioned in the Oriya literature. Here attempt has been made to discuss them on the basis of the field survey, available myths, stories, archeological materials and published booklets etc. However, the Grāmadevatīs, those are regarded as the protectress deities of the respective Hindu villages have not been taken into account. The Śākta *pīṭhas* displayed (table-1) will give a graphic picture of the development and popularity of Śākta Tāntricism in Orissa through the different ages. It may be noted that the dating of the following sacred shrines has been drawn on the basis of the architectural aspects of the monuments, iconographic features of the existing images, archaeological remains of the respective areas, literary and epigraphic evidences along with the other relevant documents.

Table 1: Table containing the list of prominent Śākta *pīṭhas* of Orissa

Sl. No	Name of the Pīṭha or centre	District	Limb of Satī	Presiding deity	Monument	Remains	Period in century AD
1	Virajā *Kṣetra*, Jājpur	Jājpur	Nāvāl portion	Mahiṣāsuramardini	*Rekhā* temple	Runis of original temple at Kalsapur	5/6th
2	De-Bhogaka *Kṣetra*, Deogāon	Kalāhaṇḍi	---	Stambheśvarī (Pillar goddess)	---	Terāsingā copper plate	5/6th
3	Bhagavatī *Pīṭha*, Bānpur	Khurda	*Mukha* (Mouth)	Bhagavatī	*Piḍhā* temple	Early remains	6/7th
4	Tārā Tāriṇī *Pīṭha*, Puruṣottamapur	Ganjam	Breasts	Tārā Tāriṇī (two pieces of stone)	Later temple	--do--	7/8th
5	Jaleśvarī *Pīṭha*, Jaseśvara	Balasore	Belley	Jaleśwarī Caṇḍī	Later temple	--do--	8/9th

6	Bhaṭṭārikā *Pīṭha*, Baḍambā	Cuttack	---	Bhaṭṭārikā	*Piḍhā*	Early remains	8/9th
7	Carchikā *Pīṭha*, Bānkī	Cuttack	---	Cāmuṇḍā	Later temple	--do--	8/9th
8	Vyāghradevī, Kuladhā	Ganjam	---	Vyāghradevī (Piece of stone)	Rock shelter	---	8/9th
9	Causaṭhī Yoginī *Pīṭha*, Hirāpur	Khurda	---	Causaṭhī Yoginīs	Circular temple	Ruins	8/9th
10	Kīchakeśvarī, Khiching	Mayurbhanj	--	Kīchakeśvarī (Cāmuṇḍā)	Reconstructed *Rekhā* temple	Śaiva and Śākta remains	8/9th
11	Sāralā *Pīṭha*, Jhāṇkaḍa	Jagatsingpur	---	Caṇḍī (Sarasvatī)	Later temple	Early remains	9th
12	Bāliharacaṇḍī, Bāliharacaṇḍī	Puri	---	Mahiṣāsuramardinī	Renovated temple on early shrine	Early remains	9th

13	Nāyāryaṇī *Pīṭha*, Diā	Khurda		Mahiṣāmardinī (Cāmuṇḍā, Vaiṣṇavī)	Later temple	Early remains	9th
14	Maṅgalā *Pīṭha,* Kākaṭpur	Puri	---	(Vaiṣṇavī) Reconstructed	*Piḍhā* temple	Early remains	9th
15	Rāma Caṇḍī *Pīṭha* Koṇārk	Puri	---	Mahiṣāsuramardini	*Piḍhā* temple	Early remains	9th
16	Nāyāryaṇī *Pīṭha*, Chilika	Ganjam	---	Mahiṣāsuramardini	*Khākharā* temple	Early remains	9th
17	Bhagavatī Pīṭha, Golabāi	Khurda	Śakti	Mahiṣāsuramardini	Later temple	Early remains	9th
18	Maṇināga *Pīṭha*, Raṇpur	Nayagarh	---	Circular object of phidic cult	Later temple	Early remains on e hill	9th
19	BhadraKālī, Bhadrak	Bhadrak	---	Kālī Renovated	temple on early shrine	Early remains	9 /10th

20	Causaṭhī-Yoginī *Pīṭha*, Rāṇīpurjhariāl	Bolangir	---	Causaṭhī Yoginīs	Circular temple	Two Other *Khākharā* temples	10th
21	Saptamātṛkā *Pīṭha*, Belkhaṇḍī	Kalāhaṇḍi	---	Saptamātṛkās	*Piḍhā* temple	Early remains	10th
22	Śākta *Pīṭha* Peḍāgaḍi	Mayurbhanja	---	Cāmuṇḍā	Ruined temple	Early remains	10th
23	Mānikeśvarī *Pīṭha* Pārlākhemuṇḍi	Gajapati	---	Mahiṣāsuramardinī	Later temple	Early remains	10/11th
24	Bhubaneswarī Ekāmra *Pīṭha*, Bhubaneswar	Khurda	*Adhara* (Lowerlip)	Gopālinī (Bhubaneswarī)	*Khākharā* temple	Other Śākta temples	11/12th
25	Kataka Caṇḍī, Cuttack	Cuttack	---	Caṇḍī	Later temple on early ruins	Early remains	12th
26	Bāṭa Maṅgalā, Puri	Puri	---	Maṅgalā	Later temple	---	12th
27	Kalijai *Pīṭha*, Chilika	Khurda	---	Kalijai	Later temple	Early remains	12th

28	Puruṣottama *Kṣetra*, puri	Puri	Foot	Vimalā	*Rekhā* temple	Śākta temples	12th
29	Tārā *Pīṭha,* Bhusaṇḍapur	Khurda	---	Ugra Tārā	Later temple	Early remains	12 /13th
30	Dakṣina Caṇḍī *Pīṭha,*Hadapada (tapanga)	Khurda	-----	Mahiṣāsuramardinī	*Khakharā* temple	Earlyremains/ inscription	13th
31	Hiṅgulā *Pīṭha*, Tālcher (Gopālprasāda)	Dhenkanal	---	Hiṅgulā	Later temple	---	13th
32	Tāriṇī *Pīṭha,* Ghatagaon	Keonjhar	---	Tāriṇī	Later temple	---	14th
33	Samaleśwarī *Pīṭha* ,Sambalpur	Sambalpur	---	Piece of stone (Pillar goddess)	Later temple	---	14th
34	Baruṇei *Pīṭha,* Khurda	Khurda	---	Aruṇei-Baruṇei	Later temple	Early remains	16th

It is ascertained from the above discussion that Orissa alias Uḍḍiyāna is one of the major Śākta *pīṭhas* of India. Among the prominent 18 *pīṭhas* of Indian sub-continent, the Śākta *pīṭha* of Kaliṅga or Uḍḍiyāna is of a great importance as illustrated by the Kulārṇava Tantra. The above cited table shows the important Śākta centers developed throughout the length and breadth of Orissa. Some of the centers rose to prominence being associated with the remains of Satī while others have gained popularity on a period of time. These Śākta centers play a vital role for the popularisation of Śakti cult in Orissa.

References

1. A. A. Macdonell, Sanskrit English Dictionary, Strassburg, 1893, p. 305.
2. Swami Tapasyananda, *Saundarya Lahari of Śrī Sankaracarya*, Ramakrishna Math, Madras, 1987, p. 27.
3. M. Monier Williams, *Sanskrit English Dictionary*, New Delhi, 2008, p.1044.
4. D.R. Rajeswari, *Śakti Iconography*, New Delhi, 1989, p.1.
5. *Devī Bhāgavata*, V, 11.6.4; IX.13.81-89.
6. As quoted by B. Srivastava, *Iconography of Śakti*, Varanasi, 1978, p.33.
7. *Devī Mahātmya,* V.12-33.
8. *Śvetāśvetara Upaniṣad*, 1.3.
9. *Kena Upaniṣad*, 3.1.
10. *IŚvetāśvetara Upaniṣad*, IV. 10.
11. *Atharvaveda*, III.9, RV. V. 84.
12. E. A. Payne, *The Śāktas*, Oxford University press, Oxford, 1933, p. 115.
13. *Ibid.*, 114
14. *Mackenzie, Indian Myth of Legend*, London, 1980, p. XXXIX.
15. V.A. Smith, *Oxford History of India*, Oxford, 1920, p.9.
16. John Marshall, *Mohenjodāro and Indus Civilization*, Vol.I, London, 1931, p.50.
17. E. Mackay, *Early Indus Civilization*, London, 1935, p. 54.
18. John Marshall, *op. cit.*, London, 1931, Vol. I, p. 49.
19. E. Mackay, *op. cit.*, p. 54.

20. J. N. Banejee, *Development of Hindu Iconography*, Calcutta, 1956, p. 188.
21. John Marshall, *op. cit.*, p.52.
22. Kalidasa, *Raghuvaṁśa* 1.1.
23. *Ibid.*
24. *Rigveda.* VI. 61.1.
25. J.N. Banejee, *op. cit.*, p. 490.
26. *Rigveda. Khila Śūkta.* X. 127.
27. *Ibid.*
28. *Śri Śūkta* (Appended to the 5th Book of the Rigveda)
29. J.N. Banejee, *op. cit.*, p. 490-91.
30. N. N. Bhattacharya, *History of Śākta Religion*, Delhi, 1974, p. 32.
31. *Vājasaneyi Saṁhitā*, III. 53.
32. *Taittiriya Brāhmaṇa*, 1.6. 10.
33. *Śatapatha Brāhmaṇa*, II. 6.2.9.
34. *Taittiriya Āraṇyaka*, X. 18.
35. *Kena Upaniṣad*, III. 25.
36. *Śvetāśvetara Upaniṣad*, IV. 10.
37. *Sānkhyāyana* Gr. S. II. 14. 1. (a); Manu s., III. 89.
38. *Taittiriya Āraṇyaka*, X. 1. 7.
39. J. N. Farkhuhar, *An Outline of the Religious Literature of India*, Oxford, 1920, p.266.
40. *Sita Upaniṣad.* 35.
41. *Rāmāyaṇa* VII. 13.23.
42. *Ibid.*, V. II. 145-168.
43. *Ibid.*, V. 3. 21-30.
44. *Ibid.*, V. 51. 34-35.
45. *Adyātma Rāmāyaṇa.* 1. 4. 18; VI. 3. 38.
46. *Kurma Purāṇa*, I. 21. 19-20.
47. *Padma Purāṇa*, V. 12. 54-67.
48. *Adhyātma Rāmāyaṇa*, V. 12. 54-67.
49. *Brahma Vaivarta Purāṇa.* III. 30. 17; III. 45. 1-76.
50. *Mahābhārata.* IV, 6.2.
51. V. R.R. Dikshitar, *The Lalitā Cult*, University of Madras, 1942, p. 27.

52. *Mahābhārata*. IV. 6.8.
53. *Harivaṁśa,* p. III. 3.7.
54. *Ibid*., 18.17.
55. *Mahābhārata*. III. 85. 119.
56. *Ibid*., III. 83. 58.
57. V.S. Agrawal, *Mārkaṇḍeya Purāṇa -A study*, Allahabad, 1961, p. 19.
58. V. S. Agrawal, *Devī Mahātmya*, Allahabad, 1963, p. 156.
59. *RigVeda*. 10.72.
60. *Sapta Śatī*. XI.42.
61. *Sapta Śatī*. V.14-16.
62. *Ibid*., IV. 7; V. 9.
63. *Ibid*., V. 14-80.
64. *Ibid*., I. 77.
65. *Devī Bhāgavata*. P. 1.1.1.
66. *Ibid*., VII. 1. 21-36.
67. *Ibid*., VI. 21. 51-52.
68. J.N. Banejee, *op. cit*., p. 495.
69. *Brahma Yāmala*, p. 184-185
70. D. R. Rajeswari, *op. cit*., p. 13.
71. *Ibid*., p. 14.
72. Thomas Donaldson and K. S. Behera, *Sculpture Masterpieces from Orissa*, New Delhi, 1988, p. 33.
73. E. Hultzsch, 'Inscriptions of Asoka', *Corpus Inscriptionum Indicarum*, Vol. I, London, 1925, p. 66.
74. B. C. Pradhan, *Śakti worship in Orissa*, Ph. D. Dissertation Sambalpur University, 1983, p. 18.
75. S.N. Rajaguru, *Inscriptions of Orissa*, vol. I, part II, Berhampur, 1958, pp. 195-6.
76. *Kathāsaritsāgara of somadeva*, tr. By C.H. Tawney, (Ed.) N.M. Penzer, London, 1924, Vol. I. pp. 102-136 and Vol. II, p. 141.
77. B. C. Pradhan, *op. cit*., p. 39.
78. *JBORS*, Vol. II, pp. 440-5; pp. 405-09.
79. K. C. Panigrahi, *History of Orissa (Hindu Period)*, Cuttack, 1981, pp. 348-9.

80. M. N. Das, (Ed). *Sidelights on Orissan History and Culture*, Cuttack, 1978, p. 351.
81. S. N. Rajaguru, *op. cit.*, pp.82-6.
82. D. C. Sircar, *The Śākta Pīṭhas*, Delhi, 1973, p.34.
83. K. C. Panigrahi, *Jājpur in the Culture and History of Orissa (Oriya)*, Jājpur, 1973.
84. A. K. Rath, *Studies on Some Aspects of the History and Culture of Orissa*, Calcutta, 1987, pp. 82-3.
85. R. P. Chanda, *Exploration of Orissa, Memoirs of the Archaeological Survey of India*, No. 44, 1930, p. 4-5.
86. *Inscriptions of Orissa*, Vol. I, part. II, p. 107; *Epigraphic India*, Vol. III, pp. 41-50.
87. Francesco Brighenti, *Śakti Cult in Orissa*, New Delhi, 2001, p. 90.
88. K. C. Panigrahi, *op. cit.*, pp. 317-18.
89. *JBORS*, Vol. 11, pp. 419-427.
90. M.P. Dash, (Ed.), *A Descriptive Catalogue of Sanskrit Manuscripts of Orissa*, Vol. V. Bhubaneswar, 1965, pp.XXXVIII-XLIV.
91. Brighenti, *op. cit.*, p. 96.
92. S. N. Rajaguru, *Inscription Of Orissa*, Vol. IV, *op. cit.*, p.87; E. I. Vol. XXVII, pp. 319-325.
93. S. N. Rajguru, *op. cit.*, Vol. IV, 1966, p. 391.
94. T. E. Donaldson, *Hindu Temple art of Orissa*, Vol.1 Leiden, 1985, p. 291-2.
95. *Ibid.*, pp. 402-3.
96. K. C. Panigrahi, *op. cit.*, (1961), p. 136; T.E. Donaldson, *op.cit.*, Vol. III, (1987) p. 1072.
97. *Ibid.*(T.E. Donaldson).
98. Brighenti, *op. cit.*, p. 134.
99. K. C. Panigrahi, *op. cit.*, p. 334.
100. Brighenti, *op. cit.*, p. 142.
101. *Ibid.*
102. A. Boner and S. R. Sharma (Eds), *Śilpa Prakāśa*, Leiden 196, p. XIX.
103. *A. Descriptive Catalogue of Sanskrit Manuscripts of Orissa*, *op. cit.*, p. XVIII.
104. *Ibid.*

105. *O.H.R.J*, Vol. I, no. 4(1953), p. 285.
106. *O.H.R.J*, Vol. XXVII, Nos.1, 2, 3 and 4, pp. 94-5.
107. N. N. Bhattacharya, *History of the Śākta Religion, New Delhi*, 1974, p. 148.
108. K. C. Panigrahi, *op. cit.*, o. 320.
109. N. N. Bhattacharya, *op. cit.*, p. 148.
110. K. C. Panigrahi, *op. cit.*, p. 141 and 179.
111. H. C. Das, *Śākta Pīṭhas: A Study*, Bhubaneswar, 1999, p.177.
112. *O.H.R.J*, Vol. VIII, No8, 3 and 4, p. 167.
113. David Kinsley, *Hindu Goddess*, Delhi, 1987, p. 184.
114. D. C. Sircar, *op. cit.*, pp. 6-7.
115. S. Bagchi, *Eminent Indian Śākta Centers In Eastern India*, Calcutta, 1980, p. 1.
116. M.P. Dash, (Ed.), *op. cit.*, p. v.
117. D. C. Sircar, *op. cit.*, p. 24.
118. M.P. Dash, (Ed.), *op. cit.*, p. VII.
119. *Ibid.*
120. T. E. Donaldson, *Tantra and Śākta Art of Orissa*, 2002, New Delhi, p. 71.
121. *Ibid.*

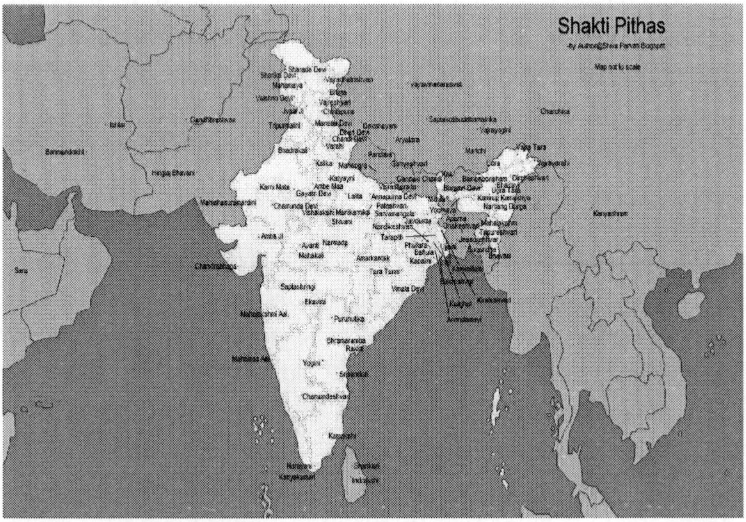

2

MĀTṚKĀS AS DIVINE MOTHERS

A band of female divinities entitled as Mātṛkās occupy an eminent place in the Hindu perception. They assume paramount significance especially in the goddess-oriented Tantric sect of Hinduism. These little Mothers are the endowed energies of the important familiar male deities. Early references to the Mātṛkās can be assigned to the first century A.D· as mentioned by David Kinsley[1] but they rarely specify their number, the implication in some passages is that they are innumerable. In the medieval period their number and names become more standardized. They are usually said to the number seven as Saptamātṛkās though some texts mention eight and sixteen[2]. Since they are generally depicted as heptads, they are called Saptamātṛkās who in the Vedas form one band and take their seat on a moving chariot symbolized as the human body or each solar ray or each octave sound. Brahmāṇī or Sarasvatī, Māheśvarī or Raudrī, Kaumārī or Kātyāyanī, Vaiṣṇavī or Lakṣmī, Vārāhī, Indrāṇī or Māhendri and Cāmuṇḍā are regarded as Saptamātṛkās[3] symbolizing the incarnation of the supreme reality. However, they may sometimes be eight as Aṣṭamātṛkās. In South India the seven female divinities are worshipped under Saptamātṛkā *upāsanā* whereas the Aṣṭamātṛkās are venerated in Nepal. The Mātṛkās are a collective of seven or eight goddesses, whose paradoxical natures express the inter relationship between the cyclical nature of women's bodies and perennial earth based rituals. They are Mother Goddesses, yet not restricted to the procreative implication of motherhood. The Mātṛkās are aspects of the Great Goddess in her full power and work together in collective form. In the *Devī-Mahātmya* myth, they appear as aspects of the Great Goddess Durgā's power, which She calls forth to aid her in the battle against the asuras, demons. They spring from Durgā's forehead riding animal mounts (goose, bull, tiger, etc.) in their most terrifying forms and successfully restore equilibrium to the threatened cosmos.

Etymologically 'Mātṛkā' is derived from the root word, Mātṛ meaning to measure or to be contained or comprised in[4]. Mātṛ, thus means a mother, who contains, 'Mā' obviously referring to the maternal potential.*Rig Veda* interprets Mātṛ as one who measures across or traverses, and as one who has true knowledge[5], meaning that of regeneration. Mātṛ also means a mother as a term of respect or endearment[6], when used generically, Mātṛkā, means all kind of groups[7] of mothers. Mātṛkā as used in the present context refers to the Śakti embodiments of respective gods as described in the Brahmanical literature, who in iconic sculptural portrayals are the divine mothers and warriors, used for ritual worship.

METAPHYSICAL SIGNIFICANCE

The seven little mothers or Saptamātṛkās represent seven great principles of manifestation such as mind, life and matter comprised of five gross elements[8]. Furthermore, the order of the Saptamātṛkā usually begins with Brāhmī symbolizing creation. It is often represented by the all-comprehensive primordial *Nāda* **Om** (*praṇava*).Then, Vaiṣṇavī provides the created world with symmetry, beauty and order. Māheśvarī, who resides in the hearts of all beings, breaths in life and individuality. Kaumārī, Guru-guhā, the intimate guide in the cave of one's heart, inspires aspirations to develop and evolve. Vārāhī is the power and aggressive intent to go after enjoyment. Indrāṇī is the sovereignty intolerant of opposition and disorder. Cāmuṇḍā is the destroyer of delusions and evil tendencies, paving way for spiritual awakening.

From the Vedic sources what appears to be more important to the Saptamātṛkās is the symbology of *heptads*. This numerical pre-figuration is often found in *Rig Veda* as a sacred number. The numerical fixations of the *Puranic* materials as group of seven goddesses are linked to the Vedic sacred number seven. The Vedic Aryans considered that the universe consisted of seven regions having seven *Ādityas*. Also the chariot of *Surya,* or Sun God in Hindu mythology, is driven by sever horses[9]. The colour of the spectrum was reinforced on the idea that seven was the basic unit of measuring life. Therefore, the connection of the *Sapta* Mātṛkās with the Vedic sources would be fundamental. In the book *Iconography of Saptamātṛkās* by Kathrine Anneharpen, she says that Babylonians, Greeks, Hibrus and Indonesians recognize number seven as sacred too. In the *Varāha Purāṇa*, however states that these mother goddesses are eight in mother and includes among them the goddess Yogeśvarī, the *Purāṇa* further says that these Mātṛkās represent eight inauspicious mental qualities[10] which are furnished below.

- Yoge*śvarī* represents *kāma* or desire
- Māheśvarī, *krodha* or anger
- Vaiṣṇavī, *lobha* or covetousness
- Brahm*āṇī, mada* or pride
- Kaumārī, *moha* or illusion
- Indrāṇī, *matsarya* or faultfinding, jealousy
- Cāmuṇḍā, *paisunya* or animal passion
- Vārāhī, *asuya* or hatredness

Besides, the Saptamātṛkās or seven mothers symbolize the composition of human body which is constituted of seven types of substances (*sapta dhātu*); seven senses (*sapta indriya*); seven energy centers including the final *Sahasrāra-chakra* (*sapta chakra*); seven phases of existence or seven states of consciousness (*Bhuḥ; Bhuvaha* ; *Svaḥ; Mahaḥ; Janaḥ; Tapaḥ* and *Satyam*) and so on.

GENESIS

According to Jagdish Narain Tiwari and Dilip Chakravati, the Mātṛkās were existent as early as the Vedic period and the Indus Valley civilization. Seals with rows of seven feminine deities or priestesses are cited as evidence for the theory[11]. A Hindu text known as the Rig-Veda (IX 102.4) speaks of a group of seven Mothers who control the preparation of Soma, but the earliest clear description appears in some layers of the epic *Mahābhārata* dated to 1st century AD[12]. Wangu believes that Mātṛkā description in the *Mahābhārata*, is rooted in the group of seven females depicted on Indus valley seals. It was assumed that the people locally worshipped these goddesses; such an example is also described in Zimmer Heinrich book *The Art of Indian Asia*, about the seven shrines of seven Mother Goddesses worshipped locally. By the fifth century, all these goddesses were incorporated in mainstream orthodox Hinduism as Tantric deities[13].David Kinsley proposes that the Mātṛkās may be non-Aryan or at least non-Brahmanical (orthodox Hinduism), local village goddesses, who were being assimilated in the mainstream. He cites two reasons for his assertion: their description in Mahābhārata as dark in colour, speaking foreign languages and living in "peripheral areas" and their association with non-Brahmanical god Skanda and his father, Shiva, who though Vedic has non-Brahmanical attributes. Sara L. Schastok suggests that Mātṛkās maybe inspired by the concept of

Yakshas, who are associated with Skanda and Kubera both are often portrayed with the Mātṛkās. In contrast to Indus valley origins theory, Bhattacharyya notes: The cult of the Female Principle was a major aspect of Dravidian religion, the concept of Śakti was an integral part of their religion. The cult of the Saptamātṛkā, or Seven Divine Mothers, which is an integral part of the Śākta religion, may be of Dravidian inspiration[14].

The Saptamātṛkās were earlier connected with Skanda (Kumāra) and in later times, associated with the sect of Śiva himself. During the Kushāṇa period (1st to 3rd century), the sculptural images of the Mātṛkās first appear in stone. The Kushāṇa images merged from the belief in Balagraha (lit "destroyers of children") worship related to conception, birth, diseases and protection of children. The Balagraha tradition included the worship of the infant Skanda with the Mātṛkās. The goddesses were considered as personifications of perils, related to children and thus, were pacified by worship. The Kushāṇa images emphasize the maternal as well as destructive characteristics of the Mātṛkās through their emblems and weapons. They appear to be an undifferentiated sculptural group but develop in standard and complex iconographic representation during the following Gupta period.

In the Gupta period (3rd to 6th century A.D.), folk images of Mātṛkās became important in villages. The diverse folk goddesses of the soldiers like Mātṛkās were acknowledged by the Gupta rulers and their images were carved on royal monuments in order to strengthen the loyalty and adherence of the armed forces. The Gupta kings Skandagupta and Kumaragupta I (c. second half of fifth century) made Skanda (Kumāra) their model and elevated the position of Skanda's foster mothers, the Mātṛkās from a cluster of folk goddesses to court goddesses. Since the fourth century, Parhari, Madhya Pradesh had a rock-cut shrine been solely devoted to the Saptamātṛkā.

The Western Ganga Dynasty (350–1000 CE) kings of Karnataka built many Hindu temples along with Saptamātṛkā carvings and memorials, containing sculptural details of Saptamātṛkās. The evidence of Mātṛkā sculptures is further pronounced in the Gurjara–Patiharas (8th to 10th century A.D.) and Chandella period (8th to 12th century A.D.). The Chalukyas claimed to have been nursed by the Saptamātṛkās. It was a popular practice to link South Indian royal family lineage to a Northern kingdom in ancient times[15]. During the Chalukya period (11th to 13th century), all Mātṛkās continued to figure among the deity sculptures of this period. The Kadambas and Early Chalukyas from the fifth century praise the Mātṛkās in their preambles, as giver of powers to defeat enemies. In most of the relevant texts, their exact number has not been specified, but gradually their number and names became increasingly crystallized and seven goddesses were identified as Mātṛkās, albeit some references indicate eight or even sixteen Mātṛkās. Laura Kristine Chamberlain (now Laura K. Amazzone) cites: The inconsistency in the number of Mātṛkās found in the valley Indus today (seven, eight, or nine) possibly reflects the localization of goddesses. Although the Mātṛkās are mostly grouped as seven goddesses over the rest of the Indian sub-continent, an eighth Mātṛkās has sometimes been added in Nepal to represent the eight cardinal directions. In Bhaktapur, a city in the Kathmandu Valley, a ninth Mātṛkā is added to the set to represent the center

MYTHOLOGY

A number of Sanskrit texts provide the detailed account of the emergence of the Saptamātṛkās. The legend of the little mothers is repeated in various texts like the *Mahābhārata*, *Varāha Purāṇa*, *Matsya Purāṇa*, *Mārkaṇḍeya Purāṇa*, *Bhāgavata Purāṇa*, *Viṣṇudharmottara Purāṇa* etc. Such legends which are associated with the combating episodes of the deities will certainly provide a clear picture about the mythological function of the Mātṛkās. In this regard the following illustrations may be taken into account which shed focus on the mythological aspects of the Mātṛkā goddesses.

Vāmana Purāṇa

Vāmana Purāṇa (Chap 56). A war took place between the Devas and the *asuras*. When the *asuras*, Chaṇḍa and Muṇḍa, were killed, another *asura* named Raktabīja entered the battlefield with chariots, elephants, horses and infantry. Seeing the large troop, *Kauśikī* and *Kāli* made a loud sound and from their mouth Māheśvarī and Brahmāṇī came out seated on a swan and wearing rosary and holding water pot in their hands. From the lion of Māheśvarī came out Kaumārī, seated on a peacock and holding a lance. Vaiṣṇavī came out from Kaumārī's hand, seated on Garuda and holding a conch, discus, club, sword, bow and arrow. From her posterior came out Vārāhī, seated on the Seshnaga (serpent), and from her heart came out *Nārasiṁhī* with fierce claws, and from her foot *Cāmuṇḍā* came out. From the eye of *Brāhmanī* came out *Māheśvarī* with three eyes, seated on bull and wearing snakes as bangles and earrings holding a trident.

THE MAHĀBHĀRATA

Regarding the origin of the Mātṛkās the following story is narrated in the *Mahābhārata*[16]. When Prahalāda, a great devotee of Viṣṇu renounced worldly life, Andhakāsura became the chief of the *asuras* (demons). By practising austerities, Andhakāsura obtained boons from Brahmā which made him very powerful, and thereafter he began to harass the gods in many ways. The helpless gods headed for Kailasa to complain to Lord Śiva who listened to them carefully. In the meantime, the *asura* chief, Andhakāsura, appeared suddenly with the intention of carrying away Pārvatī, wife of Śiva. In a fit of anger Śiva began fighting with Andhakāsura with his army of ganas. Śiva shot him with an arrow wounding him badly, blood began to flow profusely from the wound and from each drop of blood out came an Andhakāsura and there appeared thousands of *asuras* who battled against Śiva. Thereupon Indra and other gods sent their Śaktis (female powers) to kill the asuras. The Śaktis were Māheśvarī, Vaiṣṇavī, Brahmāṇī, Kaumārī. Indrāṇī, Vārāhī and Cāmuṇḍā, the female counterparts of Maheśvara, Viṣṇu, Brahmā, Kaumāra, Indra, Varāha and Yama, respectively. The seven Mātṛkās drank each drop of blood issuing from the wounds of Andhakāsura stopped further multiplication of *asuras* and finally killed him.

KURMA PURĀṆA

The *Kurma Purāṇa*[17] describes the benevolent character of the Mātṛkās. According to this text there was a problem as to what should be done with those Mātṛkās to retire them to *pātalaloka* which is the abode of Tamasic and destructive elements. Viṣṇu Nṛsiṁha was approached with it request to change their destructive nature and it was done. Since then these seven Mātṛkās have a benevolent character instead of malevolent aspects.

Īśānaśiva Gurudeva Pddhati

The Īśānaśiva *Gurudeva Paddhati*[18] narrates that the Mātṛkās were created to help Lord Śiva in his fight Andhakāsura. When the Lord inflicted wounds on Andhakā, blood began to flow profusely from his body. Each drop which touched the ground assumed the shape of another Andhaka. Thus, there were innumerable *asuras* fighting against Śiva. To stop the falling of the blood, Śiva created a goddess called Yogeśvarī from the flames issuing out of his mouth. Brahmā, Viṣṇu, Maheśvara, Kumāra, Varāha, Indra, and Yama also sent their Śaktis to help Yogeśvarī in stopping the flow of blood. Thus, in this way the Saptamātṛkās were originated.They embody the seven female potentials of the important gods. In the *Suprabhedhāgama*, the Mātṛkās are said to have been created by Brahmā in order to kill Nirrita.

MATSYA PURĀṆA

According to the *Matsya Purāṇa*[19], when Śiva shot *Pāśupata* weapon on Andhakāsura, the blood gushed from the body of that demon, thousands of Andhakāsuras sprang forth from that blood and the wound of those demons also similarly multiplied itself into hundreds of demons. Therefore innumerable demons spread all over the field. Then Śiva had to create the following Divine Mothers to drink their blood. Such divine entities were Māheśvarī, Brāhmī, Kaumārī, Mālinī, Sauparni, Vayavya, Sakri, Nairitti, Sauri, Saumya, Śiva, Duti, Cāmuṇḍā, Varuni, Vārāhī, Nārasiṁhī, Vaiṣṇavī, Chalachrehike, Satananda, Bhagananda, Picchilla, Bhagamalini, Bala, Aibala, Rakta, Surabhi-Mukhamandika, Matrinanda, Sunanda, Vidali, Sakuni, Ravati, Maearakta, Pila-Pichika, Jaya, Vizaya, Jayanti, Aparājitā, Kāli, MahāKāli, Subhaga, Durbhaga, Karali, Nandini, Aditi, Diti, Mani Mrityu, Karnamoti, Gramya, Ulooki, Ghatodari, Kapali, Vazrahasta, Pisachi, Rakshasi, Bhusundi, Sankari, Chanda, Hanguli, Putabhi, Kheta, Sulochana, Dhuma, Ekavira, Karalini, Visaladanstrini, Syama, Trijati, Kukuri, Vinayaki, Vaitani, Unmattudumbari, Sidhi, Lailihana, Kaikari, Gardhabhi, Bhrukuti, Bahuputri, Vidambini, Krauncha, Sailamukhi, Vinata, Surasa, Danu, Usā, Rambha, Menaka,

Māyā, Vichitrarupa, Kamarupa, Sangama, Mukhevila, Mangala, Mahanasa, Mahamukhi, Kaumārī, Rochana, Bhima, Sadahasa, Mohodhata, Kalaparni, Kumbhakarni, Mahasuri, Sankhini, Lamba, Pingala, Lohitamukhi, Ghantarava, Danstrala, Rochana, Gokarnika, Ajamukhika, Mahagriva, Mahamukhi, Ulkamukhi, Dhumasikha, Mohana, Kampana, Nirbhaya, Bahusalini, Sarprkarni, Ekakshi, Jyotsnamukhi, Rabhasa, Nikumbha, Rakta-kampana, Mahachitra, Chandrasena, Manorama,Matangi, Lambamekhala, Pramoda, Lanfialavati, Chitta, Chittajala, Aghavinasini, Lambaetani, Lambasta, Dirghakesi, Suchira, Sundari, Subha, Ayomukhi, Krodhini, Kutumbika, Muktika, Chandrika, Balamohini, Samanya, Mahanada, Mahodari, Mahādevī, Hunkari, Rudresi, Bhutadamani, Kundajihva, Chalajjvala, Jwalamukhi, etc., etc. They looked very terrible. They all drank the blood of these demons and were exceedingly gratified. After their bout of drinking demonic blood was over and they were no longer capable of drinking furthermore, the demons again began to multiply by leaps and bounds. Then lord Śiva went to seek the help of Viṣṇu. Then Viṣṇu, with great wrath created Sushka Revati, who in a moment drank the blood of the demons. She became more withered and dry as she drank their blood and when all the blood was drunk, the demons were completely annihilated. Afterwards, all the Divine Mothers could not curb their nature and started destruction, assuming terrific appearances. Then once again Śiva thought of Nārasiṁha and said that he had created them but unable to destroy them. Hearing there words Nārasiṁha created Vāniśvarī from his tongue, Māyā from his mind, Bhagamālinī from his private parts and also thirty two divine Mothers were created by Viṣṇu from his body. They are all auspicious goddesses. Their names are Ghantakarni, Trilokyamohini, Sarva, Sattva, Sankari, Chakrahridaya, Vyomacharini, Sankhini, Lekhani, Kamasankarshini who are the maids of Vaiṣṇavī, Sankarshini, Asvathama, Bijabhava,

Aparājitā, Kalyani, Madhudamstri, Kamalotpal and Hastika are the maids of Māyā, Asita, Sukshmahridaya, Vriddha, Vesasmadansana, Nrisimha Bhiravavilva, Garutmahridaya, Virdha, Jaya are the maids of Bhavamalini and Akarnani, Sabhata. Uttaramalika, Padmakara, Jwalamukhi, Bhishmika, Kamadhenu, Balika etc., are the maids of Revati. All of them are immensely powerful and have been created from the body of Viṣṇu. They are powerful enough to create and destroy the whole universe. The divine Mothers created by Viṣṇu subdued those created by Śiva because none could stand the flash of wrath beaming from their eyes. The Mātṛkās, who were ready to destroy the world, now took refuge of Nṛsiṁha Deva who then explained to them the whole situation. Then he advised them to protect the world along with Rudra Devī given by Śiva and along with his Mātṛkās. Mahadeva gave his divine Raudra form to the Mātṛkās created by him and He remained enshrined there amongst the Mātṛkās.

DEVĪ MAHĀTMYA

The best-known mythological account of the Mātṛkās in the medieval period is found in the third episode of the *Devī Mahātmya*[20] of the *Mārkaṇḍeya Purāṇa*. There the demons Śumbha and Niśumbha, who have usurped the Gods from their positions, are confronted in battle by the Devī. When the demon armies approach her, the male gods, who are watching from the sidelines, create Śaktis, female counterparts of themselves, to help the Devī in the battle field. Seven such Śaktis, female divinities are created, and in appearance they closely resemble the male Gods from whom they are said to arise; Brahmāṇī created from the god Brahmā, holds a rosary and water pot; Māheśvarī, created from Śiva, is seated on a bull, holds a trident, wears serpent bracelets, and is adorned with the crescent moon; Kaumārī, created from Kārttikeya, rides a peacock and holds a spear; Vaiṣṇavī, created from Viṣṇu, is seated on Garuda and holds a conch, *cakra* (discus), mace, bow, and sword; Vārāhī, created from the boar *avatara* of Viṣṇu, has the form of a boar; Nārasiṁhī, created from the man-lion *avatara* of Viṣṇu, has the form of a woman-lion and throws the stars into disarray with the shaking of her lion's mane; and Aindrī, created from the god Indra, holds a thunderbolt and is seated on an elephant (8.11-20). Charging into the fray, this group of Śaktis, collectively called the Mātṛkās (8.38, 44, 49, 62), tears into the demon army and begins to slaughter them. Along with Kāli (who is also called Cāmuṇḍā), Śivadutī (a goddess formed from the Śakti of the Devī), and the Devī herself, the Mātṛkās devastate the demons. After the battle the Mātṛkās dance, drunk with the blood of their victims (8.62). This description of the Mātṛkās is repeated with very little variation in the *Devī Bhāgavata Purāṇa* (5.28-29)

BHĀGAVATA PURĀṆA

The malevolent nature of the Mātṛkās also seems clear in several passages from the Bhāgavata Purāṇa. When the races and species of beings created by Viṣṇu are listed, the Mātṛkās are mentioned with the *uragas*, *rakṣasas*, *piśācas*, *bhutas*, and other dangerous kinds of beings[21] (2.10.37-39).22 It is difficult not to suppose that the Mātṛkās, like these other beings, are terrible in character. Elsewhere in the *Bhāgavata Purāṇa* they are mentioned with the *bhutas*, *dākinis*, *vetālas*, *pretas, piśācas*, and other malign beings as part of Śiva's army (10.63.6 ff.). Again, from the context, it appears certain that the Mātṛkās are understood as a dangerous group of goddesses. When Kṛiṣṇa kills the demoness Putana, who has tried to kill the baby god by suckling him with her poisoned nipples, the cowherd women carry out protective rites to keep Kṛiṣṇa safe from future harm. At the end of their rituals, they say: "May the *Dākinis*, the

Jatādhāris . . . the goblins, the *Mātṛs*, the *Piśācas*, etc. and other evil omens and calamities dreamt of, the slayers of the old and the young, and these and other evil spirits be destroyed, being terrified at the recital of the name of Viṣṇu"[22](10.6.27-29).

DEVĪ PURĀṆA

In the different manner the role of Mātṛkās has been delineated in the *Devī Purāṇa.* In this Text apart from the Saptamātṛkās a group of sixteen Mātṛkās and six other types of Mātṛkās are mentioned.[23]It introduces the Loka-mātara (mothers of the world), a term used in the *Mahābhārata,* in the very first chapter. Kind to all creatures, the Mātṛkās are said to reside in various places for the benefit of children[24].The text paradoxically describes the Mātṛkās as being created by various gods like Brahmā, Viṣṇu, Śiva, Indra as well as being their mothers. *Devī Purāṇa* describe a pentad of Mātṛkās, who help Ganesh to kill demons.Further, sage Mandavya is described as worshipping the Māṭrpañcaka (the five mothers) named Ambikā (Kaumārī), Rudrāṇī, Cāmuṇḍā, Brāhmī and Vaiṣṇavī and who have been established by Brahmā; for saving king Harischandra from calamities. The Mātṛkās direct the sage to perform worship of Māṭrchakra (interpreted as a *yantra* or *maṇḍala* or a circular shrine to the Mātṛkās), established by Viṣṇu on the Vindhy amountains, by meat and ritual sacrifice.

VARĀHA PURĀṆA

The account of Varāha Purāṇa represents the spiritual wisdom, the *ātmavidyā.* It states that Andhakāsura, the emblem of the darkness and ignorance is defeated by the Lord Śiva who represents the light and real knowledge, *divyajñanam.* The spirit of *vidyā* like Śiva conquers over Andhakāsura who is represented by *avidyā,* the veil of illusion. Lastly, the victory is won by Śiva who has possessed the supreme knowledge. To add more, unless the eight evil qualities *kāma, krodha, lobha, moha, mada, matsarya, asuya* and *paisunya* are brought under the control of *vidyā*, the real knowledge *or Brahmajñanam* will not be dawned upon and the *Sādhaka* or aspirant will not realize the ever blissful state like Samādhi.

In the early stages the Mātṛkās were largely viewed and feared as hordes of malicious spirits harming pregnant women and children. In the later texts they were projected as troops of female warriors of ferocious nature assisting gods and goddesses in their battles against the demons. It was under the auspicious of the Tantric and Śākta theology that the Mātṛkās were thoroughly reformed and rendered into worship-worthy benevolent mother-like goddesses of great spiritual merit.

References

1. David Kinsley, *Hindu Goddess*, Delhi, 1987, p. 151.
2. J. N. Banejee, *Development of Hindu Iconography*, Calcutta, 1956, p. 503ff.
3. Bhagwant Sahai,*Iconography of Minor Hindu and Buddhist Deities,*Abhinav Publications,Delhi,1975,p.209.
4. V.V. Bhide, *A Concise Sanskrit English Dictionary,* Chitrashala Press, Poona, 1926,p.868.
5. *Rgveda*,VII,41.4
6. V.V. Bhide,*op.cit.*
7. Monier William, *A Sanskrit English Dictionary,* Delhi, 1963,p.804.
8. D.R. Rajeshwari, Śakti *Iconography,* New Delhi, 1989,p.36.
9. V.S. Agrawall, *The Glorification of the Great Goddess,* Delhi, 1963, p.49.
10. D.R. Rajeshwari, *op.cit,* p.39.
11. Jagdish Narain Tiwari, *Studies in Goddess Cults in Northern India, with Reference to the First Seven Centuries AD*, Ph.D. diss, Australian National University, p.215-244.

12. David Kinsley,*op.cit.*
13. Heinrich Zimmer, *The Art Of Indian Asia*, Its Mythology and Transformations. Motilal Banarsidas Publication. New Delhi 2001, pp.257,135.
14. N. N. Bhattacharyya, *History of the* Śākta *Religion*, Munshiram Manoharlal Publishers Pvt. Ltd., New Delhi, 1974,p.102.
15. Dr. Suryanath U. Kamath, *A Concise History of Karnataka from pre-historic times to the present*, Jupiter books,MCC, Bangalore, 2002, p60.
16. O.P.Mishra, *Iconography of the Saptamātṛkā,* Delhi, 1989, p.2.
17. T,A.G.Rao, *Elements of Hindu Iconography*, Vol. 1, Part.II, Madras, 1914, P.381.
18. Īśānaśiva Gurudeva Paddhati, p. 9.
19. *Matsya Purāṇa*, Chap. 261, p.311ff.
20. As quoted by Kinsley, p.156.
21. Jagdish Narain Tiwari,*op.cit.*, P.180
22. *Ibid.*, p.181
23. P. Pal, *The Mother Goddesses* According to the *Devi Purāṇa* in Singh, Nagendra Kumar, *Encyclopaedia of Hinduism*, Anmol Publications, New Delhi,1997 p.1835.
24. *Ibid*, p.1844.

3

ICONOGRAPHY

In the context of Indian sculptural art, the study of iconography of the goddess Vaiṣṇavī is of immense importance. Without proper understanding of iconographic traits associated with the deity, it is not possible to appreciate correctly the ideas expressed in visual form through the medium of stone, metal or paint etc. The study of formal visual surfaces of a sculpture may or may not satisfy our visual taste, but it should be kept in mind that it is not all of a piece of art. The content of a sculpture or painting is equally important and at many a time it is more important than its outer form if one is to understand the work of art fully and in its true significance.

Iconography is a language which translates the truth of religious dogmas into forms and provides them a meaningful existence. In another sense iconography is the *vidyā* which explains the principles and the meaning of contemporary beliefs of the people as represented in the visual form[1]. As a branch of study it also deals with the delineation of special features of the icons such as the *āsanas, mudrās, bhaṅgimās*, *varṇas* etc. The term icon is derived from the Greek word 'eikon' which means a figure representing a deity. With the above meaning this word has a close parallel in Indian terms as *arcā*, *berā, vigraha* connected with *tanu* or *rupa*[2]. In Indian context this branch of knowledge had developed a very intimate contact with the human beliefs-religious and psychological and has given forms to many such feelings and emotions, which are very common to life. In broader sense the term iconography really signifies the interpretative aspect of the religious art of a country which becomes manifest in diverse ways.

Sculptures or images are sometimes very useful for shedding light on obscure periods of political or general history of a nation. The inscriptions which are sometimes carved on their pedestals contain in many cases the names not only of their donors but also those of the sovereigns during whose reign these were constructed. On some of them again, we can decipher dates which help us in the reconstruction of the little known periods of history. Further, these images act as the indicators of cultural and social traits of the people who made and worshipped them. According to T.A.G Rao "the images of the Hindu gods and goddesses are representations of the various conceptions of divine attributes. Sculpturally it may be said, the number of hands in an image represents the number of attributes belonging to the deity, and their nature is denoted by the *āyudha* held in the hand or by the pose maintained by it"[3].

While discussing the iconographical features of the goddess it may be stated that she is worshipped in many forms. "When she is worshipped as an year old baby, she is known by the name of Sandhyā, if she is conceived to be two years old she is called Sarasvatī; if of seven years age Sāmbhavī, if of nine years of age, Durgā or Bālā; of ten years of age Gaurī, of thirteen, Mahālakṣmī; and of sixteen, Lalitā. Sometimes she is named in recognition to one or other of her heroic achievements; for instance, she is called Mahiṣāsuramardinī in consequence of her having destroyed the demon Mahiṣāsura"[4]. Thus, she has been known by several names which were given to her after the attainment of a particular age or after accomplishment of a particular deed.

The goddess in one form or the other has been responsible for different heroic deeds resulting in the subjugation of different demons who became the cause of considerable violence and harassment for the gods. As a result, she assumed the different attributes, postures and vehicles during the combat with the *asuras*. According to *Puranic* accounts the goddess Mahiṣāsuramardinī emerged out of the combined energies of Brahmā, Viṣṇu, Śiva and other gods for the sake of saving the gods from the wrath of Mahiṣāsura[5]. Though she is described as Ādi-Śakti or Parā-Śakti, yet she takes various forms[6], when the exigencies of the situation so warrants. This has been precisely the reason for the emergence and development of various iconographical features of the goddesses like Mātṛkās.

General Iconography for Mātṛkās

The iconographic features of the Mātṛkās goddesses are delineated in *Āgamas, Purāṇas* and also in other texts which are illustrated below for reference. However, it is very interesting to note that the sculptural depictions of Saptamātṛkās are in no way linked to their descriptions narrated in the *Purāṇas* and other literary sources. The icons are hardly related to the narrative content. The Mātṛkās of the *Purāṇas* are invariably gruesome warrior females fighting the Demons. The ferocious, blood-drinking Mātṛkās are not referred to as mothers; nor is there a reference to their 'motherly-qualities'. The early *Balagraha* deities called as Mātṛkās in the Kushāṇa period were dangerous to children. Even the Mātṛkās associated with Skanda were inimical to children up to their age of five or sixteen. Thus, there is an obvious mismatch between the Mātṛkās described in the Purāṇas and the sculptural depictions of 'mother-goddesses' of the later periods.

It is only in the post-Gupta period and the medieval centuries the numbers, names and natures of the Mātṛkās started getting standardized. That was mainly due to the influence of the Tantra and Śākta cults. In the depictions that followed thereafter, Mātṛkās were portrayed as goddesses, radiant, graceful, benevolent and caring mothers. Each Mātṛkā came to be associated with a particular divine or mystic aspect in Tantra or Yoga. In sculptures, their motherliness was often emphasized by their playful attitude towards the children they carried on their laps. But, they held on to the weapons of war. And, yet their associated symbolisms were retained; harmony in their overall structure and countenance were ensured. The later sculptures of mother goddesses exhibit aesthetic maturity and divine charm.

Brāhmī

Brāhmī is depicted with four faces having golden colour. Her right hands are projected with a trident and *abhaya hasta* and har left hands are represented with *akṣamāla* and *varada hasta*. She is seated on a red lotus with her *haṁsa* (swan) *vāhana*. Her banner is *haṁsadhwajā*. She is decorated with yellow garment and her head is adorned with *karaṇḍa-mukuṭa*. Her placement is under a *palāśa* tree. However *Viṣṇudharmottara* describes her with six hands as quoted by Rajeshwari[7].

Māheśvarī

Maheshwari who is also known as Raudrī, is the Śakti of Śiva. She is white in complexion; and has five faces and three eyes. She is depicted with four arms; two of which are in the *varada* and the *abhaya mudrā*, while the other two hands carry the trident and *akṣamāla*. Sometimes, she is also shown holding *pāna-patra* (drinking vessel) or axe or an antelope or a *kapāla* (skull-bowl) or a serpent. Her banner as well as the *vāhana* is Nandi (bull). She wears snake-bracelets; and *Jata mukuṭa* on her head.Her abode is under *a bilva* tree[8].

Vaiṣṇavī

Vaiṣṇavī is the counter part of Viṣṇu. She is depicted with four hands being seated upon a lotus, under a *rājavrikṣa*. She is dark in complexion with lovely face and pretty eyes. She wears a bright yellow garment. Her head is adorned with *kirīṭa-mukuṭa*. She is richly decorated with ornaments generally worn by Viṣṇu. She wears the *vanamāla*, the garland of Viṣṇu. The emblem on her banner as well as her *vāhana* is Garuda. When depicted with four arms, she carries in one of her hands the chakra and in the corresponding left hand the śaṅkha; her two other hands are held in the *abhaya* and the *varada mudrā* as described in the *Devī Purāṇa* and *Pūrvakaraṇāgama*.

Indrāṇī

Indrāṇī who is the Śakti of Indra is projected with four hands having dark-red complexion being seated under the *kalpaka* tree. In two of her hands she carries the *vajra* (thunderbolt) and the Śakti; while the other two hands are represented with *varada* and *abhaya mudrā*. Sometimes, she is shown holding *aṅkuśa* (goad) and lotus. She is richly ornamented; and adorned with *kirīṭa mukuṭa*. Her *vāhana* as well as the emblem on her banner is the charging elephant.

Kaumārī

Kaumārī is the power of Kumāra or Skanda Kartikeya, the war god. She is depicted with four hands having Śakti, *kukkuṭa* or *aṅkuśa*, *abhaya* and *varada* in her hands. However, *Viṣṇudharmottara* describes her with twelve hands. She is ever youthful, representing aspirations in life. Kaumārī is shown seated under a fig tree (audumbara) riding a peacock, which is also her emblem. Her complexion is golden yellow; and is dressed in red garments. She wears garland of red flowers. She is adorned with a *mukuṭa* said to be bound with *vasika* or *vachika*. She is the light of pure truth in the hearts of the devotees.

Vārāhī

Vārāhī, who is the Śakti of Varāha Viṣṇu summarizes fivefold elements such as water, fire, earth, air and ether. Each of these elements is related to lion, tiger, elephant, horse and Garuda (bird-human) which serve as vehicles of Viṣṇu. She is depicted with head of a boar having three eyes and eight hands holding in her six hands a discus, conch-shell, mace, lotus, noose and plough; while the other two hands are represented with *abhaya* and *varada mudrā*. She is depicted as riding, alternatively, a Garuda, a tiger, a lion, an elephant or a horse being seated under *kalpaka* tree. She is the devourer of darkness.

Cāmuṇḍā

Cāmuṇḍā is often depicted as dark in colour with very emaciated body, having three eyes, sunken belly and a terrifying face with a wide grin. Her hair is abundant and thick and bristles upwards. Her abode is cremation ground. She wears a very heavy *jata-mukuṭa* formed of piled, matted hair tied with snakes or skull ornaments. Sometimes, a crescent moon is seen on her head. Her garment is the tiger skin. Cāmuṇḍā is adorned by ornaments of bones, skulls, serpents and scorpions. Her four hands are represented with *ḍamaru* (drum), *triśūla* (trident*), khaḍga* (sword) and *pāna-patra* (drink-vessel). She is riding a Jackal; or is seated on a corpse (*prēt āsana*).She is accompanied by fiends and goblins. She is surrounded by skeletons or ghosts and beasts like jackals. The jackals and her fearsome companions are sometimes depicted as drinking blood from the skull-cup or blood dripping from the severed head. However

Pūrvakaraṇāgama mentions that Cāmuṇḍā is red in colour having wide open mouth set in a terrifying face with three eyes. Her socket eyes are described as burning like flames. She has a sunken belly; and, wears on her head the digit of the moon as Śiva does. She has four arms. The black or red coloured Cāmuṇḍā is described as having four, eight, ten or twelve arms, holding a *ḍamaru* (drum), *triśūla* (trident), sword, a snake, skull-mace (*khaṭvāṅga*), thunderbolt, a severed head and pāna-patra (drinking vessel, wine cup) or skull-bowl (*kapāla*), filled with blood, an urn of fire. She wears in her ears *kuṇḍala* made of conch shell[9] (*śaṅkha-patra*). Her *vāhana* is an owl; and the emblem of her banner an eagle.

Iconography of Vaiṣṇavī

Vaiṣṇavī is the creatrix of the worlds. She manifests all in the diverse forms out of its unmanifested formless state. The power which manifests in form is regarded as Vaiṣṇavī, the Śakti of Lord Viṣṇu. The following descriptions shed light on the iconographic features of goddess Vaiṣṇavī.

Śrītattvanidhi

The fourth Mātṛkā of the *Śrītattvanidhi* list is Vaiṣṇavī[10]. She is described as the Mātṛkā with six hands showing in one of the right hands the pose of *varada* and holding a club (*gadā*) and a lotus. The two of her left hands hold a conch (*śaṅkha*), discus (*cakra*) and the last one should be in the *abhaya* pose. Her mount is Garuda. She is of blue complexion and wears a *vanamāla*

Viṣṇudharmottara

It is delineated in the *Viṣṇudharmottara* that the goddess should be represented with six hands. She carries the mace and lotus in two right hands while the third displays *abhaya*. Her left hands hold a conch, *cakra*, and display *varada*[11]. She thus holds the four conventional *āyudhas* of Viṣṇu while displaying *abhaya* and *varada* with the two added hands. She wears a *vanamāla* as one of her decorative ornaments. Her *vāhana* is man-bird Garuda.

Aṁśumadbhedāgama

THE *Aṁśumadbhedāgama* describes the Vaiṣṇavī deity as *sankhachakradhara* and *varadabhayapanini* which means the Devī should be projected with four hands holding conch, discus weapons along with *varada* and *abhaya* gestures[12]. She should be decorated with the ornaments of Viṣṇu. Her *vāhana* is Garuda.

Vāmana Purāṇa

ThE *Vāmana Purāṇa* describes that the little mother Vaiṣṇavī should be depicted with six hands. The right hands are displayed with mace, arrows and conch while the left hands are represented with discus, bow and sword. She wears a *kirīṭa-mukuṭa* and other decorative ornaments. Her *vāhana* is Garuda.

Śilparatna

The Śilparatna however describes the *āyudhas* of Devī in a different manner. The text describes that the Mātṛkā Vaiṣṇavī should be projected with four hands. The right two hands are depicted with banner (*patākā*) and conch while the left two hands are shown with *cakra* and chain (*māla*). The colour of the deity is of dark complexion. The *vāhana* is Garuda.

Pūrvakaraṇāgama

The *Pūrvakaraṇāgama* mentions that the goddess Vaiṣṇavī should have lovely face with four hands. The right two hands are represented with mace and conch while the left two hands carry discus and lotus. She wears a *vanamāla* like Lord Viṣṇu and her *vāhana* is Garuda. She is seated under *rājavrikṣa.*

Devī-Mahātmya

The *Devī-Mahātmya* section of the *Mārkaṇḍeya Purāṇa* describes that the Devī Vaiṣṇavī who is the counter part of Lord Viṣṇu should be represented with four hands. The right two hands hold mace and conch while the left two hands are represented with *cakra* and bow. She wears the favourite ornaments of the Lord Viṣṇu and her *vāhana* is Garuda. The *Devī Purāṇa* closely follows the same interpretation of the *Devī-Mahātmya.*

Matsya Purāṇa

The *Matsya Purāṇa* describes the āyudha*s* and gestures of the MātṛkāVaiṣṇavī with slight deviation. Here the text states that the deity should be shown with four hands. Her two right hands are displayed with mace and conch while her left two hands are represented with *cakra* and child. The Devī is seated on a throne. She wears a *kirīṭa-mukuṭa* and other decorative ornaments.

Śāradātilaka Tantra

It is delineated in the Śāradātilaka Tantra that the Mātṛkā Vaiṣṇavī should be depicted with four hands. Her right two hands are displayed with discus and bell while her left two hands are shown with vessel and conch. She is of black complexion. In this text the *āyudhas* are described in a different manner.

Thus it is ascertained that the goddess Vaiṣṇavī is either four-armed or six-armed. When four-armed she may hold four āyudha*s* or she may hold two *āyudhas* with other two hands displaying *abhaya* and *varada*. Exceptions appear in the *Rūpamaṇḍana* where she holds three *āyudhas* with a *mudrā* replacing the lotus and in *Matsya Purāṇa* where a child replaces the lotus. In the *Agni Purāṇa*, the *Aparājitapṛcchā*, the *Devī Purāṇa* and the *Pūrvakaraṇāgama*, she holds the conventional four Vaisnava *āyudhas* while the *Devī-Mahātmya* the bow *sāraṅga* replaces the lotus[13]. In the *Mayamata* the iconography is nearly identical, though the *mudrās* and *āyudhas* are reversed, and her tree is *pipal*[14]. Moreover, the *Devī-Mahātmya* describes that the *vāhanas*, the dress, the ornaments and weapons of the Mātṛkās are similar to their counterparts[15]. The iconographic representations of Mātṛkās, however, lost much of their significance and position in the popular religious practices during the middle centuries. But, they continued to appear in temple panels and niches. Today, they linger on the fringes of the Hindu pantheon.

References

1. Sanjaya Kumar Mahaptra, *Mahiṣāsuramardinī in Art, Iconography and Cult Practices*, Agam Kala Prakashan, Delhi,2014, p.109.
2. J.N. Banerjee, *The Development of Hindu Iconography*, University Press, Calcutta, 1941, p.1.
3. T.A.G. Rao, *Elements of Hindu Iconography*, Vol.I, part.I, Madras, 1914-15, p.27.
4. *Ibid.*, vol.I, part.II, pp.332-333.
5. *Mārkaṇḍeya Purāṇa*, Canto LXXXII-Vp, 19.1.
6. *Kālikā Purāṇa*, Ch. 58.51.
7. D.R.RAJESHWARI, Śakti *Iconography*,New Delhi, 1989, P.40.
8. *Ibid.*, P.41.
9. Sanjaya Kumar Mahapatra,*Camunda in Mythology, Art and Iconography*, Delhi, 2015, p.67.
10. Balaram Srivastava, *Iconography of* Śakti,Chaukhambha Orientalia, Varanasi,1978,p.81.
11. T.A.Gopinath Rao, Elements of Hindu Iconography, Madras, 1971, p.384.

12. Balaram Srivastava, *op.cit*, p.82
13. Thomas E. Donaldson, *Tantra and* Śākta *Art of Orissa*,Vol.I, New Delhi, 2002, p.344.
14. *Mayamatam*, II. P.875.
15. Devī Mahtmya, Viii, 13-23

Head-Gear

4

SCULPTURAL REPRESENTATION

The worship of Saptamātṛkā appears to be one of the most ancient and popular cults of India as clearly indicated by the existence of a large number of Saptamātṛkā images in their various stages of preservation. Evidently this cult was widely prevalent during the early centuries of the Christian era. We may trace its origin from the Indus valley civilization, where on a seal we find seven figures standing almost in a dancing pose beside a tree. The discovery of a number of Mātṛkā sculptures is a great significance for the art and cultural history of our sub-continent. A comprehensive study of the sculptural representation will definitely shed light on the wide spread mother worship in India. The mythological and *Puranic* origin of Saptamātṛkās is not unknown to scholars but when and how they appeared in sculptures is a problem before us and for this we feel it safe to depend on archaeological sources rather on *Puranic* or traditional accounts.

Evolution in Indian Art

The early Kushāṇa images representing Saptamātṛkās are either standing or seated in *bhadrāsana* with their right hands held in *abhaya mudr*ā and the left one holding *kamaṇḍalu*. They are shown as simple female figures without any distinguishing symbols or vehicles. Their medieval traits are not yet depicted. The further evolution of the images of Saptamātṛkās is to be marked in the representation of a child in each one's lap in various attitudes. Soon, however, the distinguishing features of the seven mothers were introduced in the form of different animals and beads of birds for different divinities. Still these figures carry a child in their left lap and the right hand is held in the *abhaya mudrā*. In the last stage of their evolution all the Mātṛkās, were distinguished by different vehicles and attributes.

In the medieval period the Divine mothers are either carved together in a group or independently as one or two deities on a pedestal. The number of Mātṛkās also varies, being from three, seven, eight and even sixteen in the various texts. This happened because of the increasing importance of the Mātṛkās in society. However, the iconographic texts give us the detailed description for seven Mātṛkās viz. Brahmāṇī, Māheśvarī, Kaumārī, Vaiṣṇavī, Vārāhī, Indrāṇī and Cāmuṇḍā. The Saptamātṛkās are often engraved in relief on the lintels of the doors of the temples in a particular order flanked by Virabhadra and Ganeśa. In the depiction of the Mātṛkā images we also find some departure from the prescribed iconographic rules as is found in the case of Ellora figures[1]. All are having single face. They are distinguished only by their *lanchhanas* or emblems and their weapons. But the images of Belur have been made according to the direction given in the *Mārkaṇḍeya Purāṇa*[2].

The Gangadhara stone inscriptions of Visvavarmana a feudatory of Kumara Gupta I dated A.D. 423-24, indicates that his minister built a temple of Divine Mother[3]. In the Udaigiri caves and Badoh Pathori rock cut caves (Vidisha) belonging to the early Gupta period we get the representation of Aṣṭaśaktis and also the independent Mātṛkā images. Here the Mātṛkās are referred to, no doubt, but their exact number is not given nor does it give their respective names. However, in the early inscription of the Chalukya king, they are spoken of as the descendants of Hariti nurtured by the seven Mothers. It is thus clear that as early as A.D. 423-25 the Saptamātṛkās became special objects of worship along with the tutelary deities of the feudatories of the Gupta as also of the early Kadambas and the Chalukyas. It may also be seen that Imadpur metal images have only three Mātṛkās. Hence we suppose that in the beginning, there were only three Mātṛkās from which the number rose to seven and then to eight and in still later age, as Utpala informs, the number rose to sixteen. The Chalukyas of Badami worshipped the Saptamātṛkās, all their inscriptions also support this statement. It is not surprising, therefore that in their temples at Aihole, the Mātṛkās should play an important role in the sculptural themes. The best example is provided by Ravana-Phedi where they are seen standing in the left chamber of the *maṇḍapa*. Tara-basappa has a loose slab on which the Mātṛkā panel is carved. A similar slab is found in the Huchchimali temple. The seven Mātṛkās are flanked by Śiva on the right and Ganeśa on the left, their vehicle carved below on the pedestal.

Sculptural representation of the Saptamātṛkās is found in a few places in Tamilnadu. The earliest is in the Kailasnath temple at Kanchipuram (Chingleput district) and is dated c. 720 A.D.[4]. Traces of ancient temple of Saptamātṛkās are noticeable in a few places, but the original structures do not exist at present. However, the earliest Saptamātṛkā temple may be identified at Alampakkam (Lalguditaluk of Tiruchirapalli dist.). The original structure may be assigned to the period of the Pallava king, Dantivarman on the basis of a Chola inscription found at the basement of the *vimāna*. The *vimāna* of the temple was renovated during the time of Aditya I and so the present structure cannot be dated to the Pallava time. A few Chola inscriptions refer to the worship of the Saptamātṛkās. Similar representations of the Mātṛkās appear around the *mukhasālā* doorway of the Singhanath temple.

On the rock at Tirahi gate in Ajaigarh fort there is a row of eight goddesses of whom seven are sitting and one standing. Their names are written below the images. From Bheraghat (Jabalpur) among the Yogini figures, eight have been identified as Aṣṭamātṛkās or female energies of the gods. In Konch temple[5] some eighteen miles from Gaya the representation of *Aṣṭaśakti* is found. In Lakhamandala is found a black stone slab depicting seven Mothers in relief[6]. At one end is Lakulisa and the other Ganeśa. There is also one Māheśvarī on a fragmentary seal of early period and a relief of Nārasiṁhī from Satna. Another seal of burnt clay is depicted with Brahmāṇī[7]. A very fine sculptured slab, representing the *Aṣṭaśaktis* with their symbols the bull, the duck, the lion, the bird, the elephant and a prostrate human figure has been discovered. In the temple at Chatagi near Bijapur a slab representing the seven mothers is built in the interior of the *maṇḍapa*. Saptamātṛkā along with nine planets are found on the door jambs of Mahadeo temple at Kodal in the Damoh district dated 12th century A.D. Excavations at Ahichhatra have revealed a Mātṛkā temple and several images of the Mātṛkās. Some specimens of the existence of this cult in Goa are present even now, which date back to the reign of the Kadamba rulers. The representation of the Saptamātṛkās at Ellora again points to the popularity of this cult but all these specimens date back to 8th century A.D. and later periods. Saptamātṛkā sculptures have been noticed from the South, the Western Ghats, and in States as far as and in between Orissa, Madhya Pradesh, Gujarat, Rajasthan and Himachal Pradesh. Every where the panels had a local character and conventionally in and around them. But in Baroda regions we see them in standing posture in a very rhythmic manner and feminine charm. They have been beautifully executed. It is a dramatically effective adaptation of the woman holding a child with the right arm, providing a full support of her hip, in a twisting gesture, the thrust of the body and limbs is conceived with wonderful intuitive sense of sculpture[8].

The existence of Saptamātṛkā in standing posture has been reported from Rajasthan. These images also belong to the earlier period of 7th and 8th century A.D. and to the subsequent period. The Saptamātṛkā panels were very common in those days in almost all the temples in Rajasthan around Jodhpur area. We have figures of them from Mandor and from Badoli where there is a huge though unfortunately broken *toraṇa* lying in the enclosure, which has the panel of these eight divine mothers. It is quite possible that the Saptamātṛkā cult could have reached Rajasthan from South and East as some scholars believe. In Rajasthan area, both the Saptamātṛkās as well as the Aṣṭamātṛkā: group worship has been prevalent. There is one more addition which is Yogeśvarī with a child on her lap. There are also the Vārāhī and Indrāṇī of the panel having a child held in their laps. Some stone sculptures of the Mātṛkās have been discovered from Devangana, Jagat and other places of Rajasthan. These date backs to the 7-8th century A.D. All of them identical in size and style are made of grayish stone and are in a state of good preservation.

Saptamātṛkā panels of medieval period have been brought to light from Uttar Pradesh and Madhya Pradesh. In the Museum of Uttar Pradesh there are about half a dozen sculptures that correspond almost faithfully to the description of the texts. A slab containing the Saptamātṛkās is discovered in Allahabad which is assigned to the early medieval period and it depicts the mother in a dancing form. The panels of Saptamātṛkās are also worth mentioning from the Museums of Madhya Pradesh, Indore, Gwalior and Rajgarh, etc. These sculptures are ascribed to the early medieval period.

Evolution in Odishan Art

As regards their representation on stones the earliest images of Saptamātṛkās are found, carved in the Projecting rock near the village Ghoral in the Titilagarh subdivision of the Bolangir District. Mr. Beglar who visited this area during the year 1874-75 and 1875-76, had wrongly identified these, figures with the Navagrahas[9].The figures were identified with the figures of Saptamātṛkās with their two associates Ganeśa and Virabhadra in the year 1953. The figures were rudely carved and have been mostly obliterated due to weathering effect. They may be tentatively assigned to the 7th century A. D. There is a very old temple of Saptamātṛkās at Bhubanesvar, not very far away from the main gate of the Liṅgarāja temple. This was noticed by Late M. M. Ganguly who has mentioned the temple as follows. 'On the *Kumbha* of the *Jungha* it may be noted is seen a *dori* or bead, similarly met with in the temple of Saptamātṛkās near the temple of Liṅgarāja[10]. But during the course of the last twenty years this notably dilapidated monument dedicated solely to the worship of Saptamātṛkās has gone out of existence due to reckless dismantling of old structures.

The next early representation of Saptamātṛkās are to be found in the lowest panel of the *bada* of the *Jagamohana* of the temple of Paraśurāmeśvara, which is slightly recessed and divided into compartment by decorated pilasters. Within these compartments along with other deities of the Brahmanical pantheon the Mātṛkā goddesses have also been represented with their two associates Virabhadra and Ganeśa. The Lord Ganeśa has got no mount here and presents a unique feature having a human visage with trunk of an elephant attached to the chin. Next to Ganeśa we find Cāmuṇḍā in her most terrific form holding trident, vase and *vīja-pūraka* as attributes. The drooping breast, sunken belly and on the whole its emaciated body are the noteworthy features of its representation. The representation of this figure differs in many respects from the later group of representation of Cāmuṇḍā. First we do not find a snake over the head of the mother which is invariably found in the later group of its representation. Secondly in the pedestal we find an owl, but not a corpse eaten by jackals. Mātṛkā Vārāhī occupies the next compartment and has been represented with a lotus and a fish in the right hands and a *kuthāra* and a vase in the left, the next deity Indrāṇī of the Paraśurāmeśvara temple is being represented with its usual mount elephant and it holds a *vajra* in the left and vase in the right. The goddess Vaiṣṇavī has been represented with the usual attribute of Viṣṇu and Kaumārī holds a *vīja-pūraka* in the right hand and with a *gadā* and *padma* in the left. The next figure may be indentified with the figure of Brāhmī who holds an *akṣamāla* and *vīja-pūraka* in the right hand, a flower and a vase in the left.

Besides, we find the representation of Mātṛkā images in the temple of Vaital which may be assigned to the 8th century A. D. A group of Saptamātṛkā headed by Virabhadra begins in the eastern wall and ends in the centre of the western wall. The presiding deity and the image enshrined in the central niche is an eight armed Cāmuṇḍā and has been depicted in her most terrific aspect, which is suggested by her sunken eyes, the hood of a snake on her head and a corpse under her feet with a jackal dragging it. Since the deity is always covered with a piece of cloth her other terrific aspects cannot be studied. All the Mātṛkās including Virabhadra and except the presiding deity Cāmuṇḍā have certain characteristics common to them all. They are all seated in *yog*āsana with full blown lotus, and at their top we find two flying *gandharvas*. A halo surrounds the head of each deity. The Saptamātṛkā headed by Virabhadra which begins in the Eastern wall have been arranged in the order of Virabhadra, Brahmāṇī, Māheśvarī, Kaumārī, Nārāyaṇī, Vārāhī, Indrāṇī and Cāmuṇḍā. No peculiarity is to be noted in the representation of the Mātṛkā deities of Vaital temple except in the representation of Nārāyaṇī or Vaiṣṇavī who has not been shown with *vāhana* Garuda in the pedestal but we find a human figure with her left hand upraised. The other attributes of Vaiṣṇavī namely *śaṅkha*, *cakra* and *gadā* are found in her hands. In the Mohini temple of Bhubaneswara the presiding deity Cāmuṇḍā is installed. This ten-armed Cāmuṇḍā is very terrific to look at however no other Mātṛkā image except Cāmuṇḍā is reported here.

Next in order of chronology may be placed the Saptamātṛkā figures of Belkhandi in the Kalahandi District. The Mātṛkās have been arranged near the western wall in the following order:—Kaumārī, Māheśvarī, Brahmāṇī, Vaiṣṇavī, Vārāhī and Cāmuṇḍā. This group resembles in every respect, the well known Saptamātṛkā statues standing on the Daśāśvamedhaghāṭ of the river Vaitaraṇī at Jajpur and those on the Mārkaṇḍeśvara tank at Puri in Orissa. On the basis of its style it is believed that the sculptures at Belkhandi may be ascribed to the Somavaṁśī period[11]. This new discovery of Saptamātṛkā temple in this unexplored valley of Tel river throws a flood of new light on the cultural and religious history of this region known as Kosala and helps us in tracing the missing link in the history of Kosala and Utkala. Another set of Saptamātṛkā is noticed in the temple of Muktesvara at Bhubanesvar. Considerable ingenuity and artistic skill have been displayed in the arrangement here have been conceived in the form of a canopy with an eight petalled lotus at the centre, each petal being occupied by a deity. The main characteristic of the representation of the Mātṛkās except Cāmuṇḍā hold babies in their arms, which in this respect agree with their counter parts discovered at Jajpur and Puri.

Relics of two seats of Saptamātṛkās now survive at Jajpur, one set consisting only two colossal figures of Vārāhī an Indrāṇī and the other set of life size figures of the mothers, five of which are now installed in a modern shrine of Vaitaraṇī. All these figures have been carved out of chlorite schist. Mr. R. P. Chanda remarks. "The most remarkable feature about these Jajpur images of the mothers is that they disclose keen sense solid masses a group of three dimensional relations on the part of their authors[12]. Mr. Chanda has assigned these images to the 8th century.A. D.

But the association of babies with the figures of Mātṛkās appears to be a later iconographic feature, which probably appeared for the first time in the temple of Muktesvara, which may be assigned to the beginning of the Somavaṁśī rule. Mātṛkā worship received a great impetus during the period of the Somavaṁśī kings and it is just probable that this new conception of association of babies in the arms of the mothers might have been initiated during their epoch. Similar set of Mother Goddesses is found in the sacred tank at Puri known as Markandeya Sarovara and five of these images have been illustrated by Dr. J. N. Banerjee[13]. The mothers made of chlorite schist very much resemble the Jajpur mothers in type. The faces of the Jajpur mothers show natural expression but the Puri mothers while holding and caressing the child with their right lower hands in exactly the same manner as their sisters of Jajpur, are themselves lost in meditation[14]. On the basis of the distinctive traits the Mātṛkā images of this place may be assigned to the same period of Somavaṁśī rule. In *Mādalāpānji* we get the mention of a name of a king known as Bhimakesari, who installed seven sisters on the eastern side of the Mārkaṇḍeśvara tank[15]. There was also a temple of m near the Alaka River in the village of Sanlapur under the Jagatsinghpur Police station in the Cuttack district. All the images are found in sitting posture holding a child on their laps. Thus they resemble the images found in the Vaitaraṇī valley and Mārkaṇḍeśvara group of Puri. All the images are here in a good state of preservation, except the figure of Vaiṣṇavī, the head of which is missing. The figures are of real objects of art. The several ornaments have been beautifully displayed and the introspective look on the face of the figures has been beautifully shown by the artists. Belonging to the same group, the figures of Saptamātṛkās from Dharmasala which are now found in the State Museum are worthy of note. Only the images of Vaiṣṇavī, Vārāhī, Indrāṇī and Cāmuṇḍā are brought to the Museum which are artistically displayed. All the figures except Cāmuṇḍā with babies in their arms have lost in meditation, and in this respect they very much resemble the figures of Mātṛkā of Mārkaṇḍeśvara tank at Puri. It is very probably that both the groups are contemporary to each other.

In a temple at Shergarh of the district of Balasore there is a unique plaque of Hara-Pārvatī carved in chlorite stone over the lintel of the temple containing the figure of Gajalakṣmī. In the lower panel of that plaque below Hara-Pārvatī the images of Cāmuṇḍā, Vārāhī, Kaumārī, Māheśvarī, Viravadra, Brahmāṇī, Vaiṣṇavī, Pārvatī and Ganeśa are found. This temple can tentatively be assigned to the 1st part of the 13th century A.D.

Apart from the temples of Mohini and Vaital at Bhubaneswar where Cāmuṇḍā is the presiding deity, there is also another temple at Khiching in the Mayurbhanj district where also the presiding deity is a Cāmuṇḍā. Since the image is always covered with a piece of cloth, it is not possible to study the outer anatomical features of the figure. In the same temple of Khiching there is also a figure of four-armed Vaiṣṇavī with Garuda beneath her seat, is a real object of art. The Goddess gracefully holds the *cakra* and *śaṅkha* in her back hands; her front right hand is represented with the *abhaya* pose while the child is shown in her front left hand. The several ornaments, including the artistic crown are tastefully displayed.

In the Prachi valley, there is a temple of Vārāhī, at Chaurasi near the village of Tulasipur. The special feature of the temple is that its *jagamohana* resembles that of Paraśurāmeśvara temple at Bhubaneswar where as the main temple is a replica of the Gouri temple of Bhubaneswar. The presiding deity Vārāhī is a two-armed beautiful image with a fish in one hand and a pot in the other hand. This temple can be definitely assigned to the Bhauma cultural age. In addition to, the Vārāhī images are also found at Pedagadi and Ayodhya. Here the Devī holds a fish and a *kapāla* in her front hands while her uplifted back hands hold a club and a noose. Her coiffure is a *sarpamukuṭa* secured by a cord[16].

Thus the powerful and innovative images of the seven mothers started appearing in various sculptures in our sub-continent. Saptamātṛkās, as a group, were depicted as beneficent goddesses but yet associated with fearsome aspects. In their individual portrayals only their benevolent aspects were projected.

References

1. T.A.G. Rao, *Element of Hindu Iconography*, Vol I., Madras, 1914-16, p. 389.
2. J.N. Banerjea, *Development of Hindu Iconography*, Calcutta,1956, p. 505
3. J.F. Fleet. *Corpus Inscriptionum Indicarum*, Calcutta, 1968, pl. 50-58.
4. K.V. Saundararajan, and Sri S. Nivasana, S. Nidhi, K.R., Srinivasanu *festschrift*, pp. 257-60.
5. A.S.I.R., Vol. VIII, pp. 72-73.
6. J.N. Banerjea, *op.cit.*, p. 186
7. *Ibid.*, p. 186
8. O.P.Misra, *Iconography of Saptamātṛkā*, Delhi, 1989,P.10
9. *Archaeological Survey of. India*, Vol. XIII, p. 138.
10. M. M. Ganguly, Orissa and her remains, p-137.
11. *J. K. H. R. S.* Vol. II p. 168.
12. *Journal of the Royal Society of Art.* Aug, 17. 1934, p. 1016.21, Memo. Arch. S. I., No. 44. p. 14.

13. *Development of Hindu Iconography*, Plates XLIII Fig. 1 3 5 Plate - XLIV Fig. 3 & 4.
14. *Journal of Royal Society of Arts*, Aug. 17, 1934 p. 1016.
15. *Mādalāpānji* (Prachi edition) p, 19.
16. T E. Donaldson, *Tantra and Śākta Art of Orissa*, Delhi, Vol.I, 2002, p.376.

5

INTERPRETATION OF IMAGES

The goddess Vaiṣṇavī, one of the benign aspects of the Divine Mother, has been described both as a Mātṛkā and Yogini in the Indian literature. She is invariably displayed in the Saptamātṛkā panels hailing from various archaeological sites of India. It is proposed to furnish a short account of prominent Vaiṣṇavī images found elsewhere of the sub-continent which will enrich the cultural heritage and sculptural art of India. It is to be noted that the sculptors of our land have presented the Vaiṣṇavī images starting from four-armed to the variety of six-armed. In this chapter an humble attempt has been made to survey the extant Vaiṣṇavī images of India which will shed light on the developmental aspect of iconic motifs.

Depiction in Indian Art

A four-armed interesting Vaiṣṇavī image is preserved in the Alampur Museum of Andhra Pradesh. Here the deity is seated in the *ardhaparyaṅka* posture. She is represented with *cakr*a in her upper right hand while the upper left hand is displayed with *śaṅkha*. The *āyudhas* in the lower right is either a fruit or vase which is obscure. The lower left hand rests on her lap.

She has been decorated with ornaments like *mukuṭa, kuṇḍala, hāra, vājū-bandha, kaṅgan*, etc. Her hair is beaded into knots. She wears a *kirīṭa-mukuṭa* on her head. Her *vāhana* Garuda is shown below her legs. Artistically it may be placed in circa 7th century A.D. (Plate.1)

The Vaiṣṇavī sculpture of Devangana, Rajasthan is shown in seated posture holding conch, discus along with *abhaya* and *varada mudrās* in her all four hands. She has been decorated with usual ornaments. Her *vāhana* is shown near her right leg. This is craved in the style of the 7th or 8th century A.D. Other post Gupta and early medieval sculptures of Vaiṣṇavī are found at Amjhera[1], Idar, now in the Baroda Museum. Another Vaiṣṇavī sculpture has been reported from district Guntur, Andhra Pradesh of this period. Due to its defaced condition details are not clear, but she is depicted in *ardhaparyaṅka* posture[2]. The extant front right hand is displayed with *abhaya mudrā* and the back left hand is shown with a *śaṅkha*. She wears a *kirīṭa-mukuṭa* on her head. This image may be ascribed to the 7th century A.D.(Plate.2)

Seated Vaiṣṇavī has been reported from Tiruchatturai of Tanjaur,Madras. Here the deity is seated in *ardhaparyaṅka* pose on a high pedestal. She is displayed with *cakra* and *śaṅkha* in the upper hands while the lower right hand is shown with *abhaya mudrā* the lower left hand rests on the lap. She wears usual ornaments but *stanapaṭṭa* of this Mātṛkā is remarkable. Her *vāhana* is not clear. This piece of sculpture is withered in condition. It may be assigned to 9th century A.D[3]. (Plate.3)

The sculpture of *Vaiṣṇavī* are preserved in various museums of Madhya Pradesh viz. Central Museum Khajuraho, State Museum, Bhopal,Central Museum Indore, Central Museum Gwalior, District Museum Rajgarh, local Museums Bhanpura, Harisingh Gour Museum, Sagar, and Reserve collection Langi

(Balaghat) etc, of different periods. These are displayed with her all attributes and usual ornaments.

The goddess Vaiṣṇavī in *tribhaṅga* posture is shown in a niche of Raisen of Ashapuri province now it is shifted to the Birla Museum[4]. She is eight armed, with her right upper most hand she holds a *ghanṭā* and in second right hand *aṅkuśa* and the third hand is shown in the *abhaya mudrā*. With the fourth hand she holds a *gadā*.The objects like *karṇaphula, hāra, bangles*, have been tastefully engraved. She wears a *kūcha-bandha* and a long thick *vanamāla*. The *Prabhāvalī* is plain. The facial expression of the deity appears to be kind and benevolent motherly and the countenance wears a sweet smile. The devotee on each side of the goddess is shown in *añjalī-mudrā*. On either side, at the top are flying *vidyādharas*. A lady on the right side with a lipstick having a round face, thin waist and long legs and like other two figures are indicative of the typical Paramara features and may be placed circa 10th century A.D. as described by O.P.Misra in the book *Iconography of theSaptamātṛkās*[5], page no 80.

A four-armed Vaiṣṇavī has been discovered from Bheraghat of Jabalpuri. This image is shown seated on a double petalled lotus in *latitāsana* with her left leg bent across the seat and the right hanging down and placed on the right palm of the Garuda seated on the pedestal below. All the hands of the goddess from the elbows and the upper part of her head from the nose upward are mutilated. Her right knee is also partly damaged. She is shown wearing *śāri* from waist downward indicated by wavy bands, *graiveyaka* with *ekāvalī, stanahāra, keyūra, mekhalā* with loops and pendants, *nūpura, vanamāla* and rings in the fingers of legs. Below the lotus seat of the goddess is a kneeling Garuda with his right leg thrown backward and the left stretched forward. He is supporting the right foot of the central deity on the palm of his right hand and his left hand is under the knee of the goddess as if supporting it. He is having beard, moustaches and his eyes are protruding. His hair is combed backward to form a semicircle of *kuṇḍalas* behind his head. The Garuda is shown wearing dhoti up to thigh which is tied at the waist with a chord, having loops and pendants. His other ornaments consist of a *hāra* of snake, *vakṣa-bandha* tied with a *cakra*, *kaṭaka* and *yajñasūtra*. On each side of the Garuda at the end of the pedestal a male figure may be seen seated on a cushion holding a *vīṇā* in his hand. The head of these two figures are mutilated. On each side of the lotus thrown of a goddess a female garland bearing attendant may be seen standing wearing the usual dress and ornaments. The face of the attendant on the right is mutilated. The middle section of the Stella flanking the two sides of the deity contains the motifs of part on the inner side and that of *gajaśārdūla* on the outer. There is lotus nimbus behind the head of the Central deity. On the right of the lotus nimbus part of the usual *gandharva* couple may be seen. The remaining part of the uppermost section of the Stella is missing. Inscription on the pedestal reads Śri Vaiṣṇavī. It is carved on dull greenish-yellow sand stone. The state of preservation is all the hands, the face and head of the central deity part of the middle and the upper section of the Stella and some of the figures carved on the remaining section of the Stella are mutilated. It may be dated as 10th century A.D[6].

An interesting sculpture of Vaiṣṇavī reported from Baijnath, Almora[7] shown in *lalitāsana*. Her four hands are represented with discuss, conch, lotus and fourth is shown in *varada mudrā*. The deity is decorated with various ornaments like *kirīṭa-mukuṭa,* ear-rings, necklace*, vanamāla, kaṅkaṇa*, *keyūra, aṅgada, kaṭisūtra* and with *prabhāmaṇḍala* on her back side of her head. Another of the same interest, the deity is now preserved in the Bharat Kala Bhawan, Varanasi, wearing usual ornaments and *Gadā* in the back right back hand. Another

Vaiṣṇavī image whose head is broken is preserved in the Central Arch. Museum of Gwalior. The upper hands are also broken but the lower right hand holds an object which is not identified while the lower left hand is either shown with *kumbha* or a vase. The *vāhana* Garuda is noticed beneath. The devotees with *añjalī-mudrā* are found on the either lower side of the deity. This image may be ascribed to the 11th century A.D. (Plate.4)

Vaiṣṇavī in high ornamentation has been reported from Siron (Latitpur). Here the Devī seated in the *ardhaparyaṅka* pose. She is shown with four hands. The upper right hand is displayed with *śaṅkha* while the upper left hand is shown with *cakra*. The objects held in the lower hands are obscure. Her right breast is chopped off. She wears ornaments like *kirīṭa-mukuṭa*, *kuṇḍala, hāra*, pendant, *vājū-bandha, kaṅgan, ekāvalī, kaṭisūtra*. Her *vāhana* Garuda is shown in human form beneath the seat. This sculpture is very graceful to look at. The goddess is placed in a niche of the temple who receives offerings from the devotees. Artistically it belongs to 11thcentury. A.D[8]. (Plate.5)

An interesting sculpture is recovered from Hinglajgarh, Mandsaur. It is now displayed in Central Museum, Indore[9]. Here the goddess is provided with four hands and she holds the āyudha*s* like the *gadā, cakra* and *śaṅkha*, her smiling face and *kūcha-bandha* are highly attractive. It is carved on sand stone. It can be assigned to the 11th century A.D.

A seated Vaiṣṇavī is notice at the Patna Museum[10], Bihar. This image is depicted with four hands holding *chakra* and *gadā* in upper right and left hands and in left lower hand she holds a baby in her lap. She is decorated with *mukuṭa*, ear-rings, *hāra* with pendant *vājū-bandha*, *kaṭi-mekhalā*, *nūpura*, etc. Her *vāhana* is shown on the *pādapiṭha*. Artistically, it may be dated to 12th century. A.D.

Another Vaiṣṇavī deity with four hands is preserved in the reserve collection at Langi (Balaghat)[11]. She is depicted in *ardhaparyaṅka āsana*. She wears ornaments like *mukuṭa*, *kuṇḍala*, beaded *hāras*, bangles, etc. It is carved on a *śilapaṭṭa* of sand stone. The Vaiṣṇavī sculpture preserved in the Archaeological Museum at Gwalior cannot be overlooked. Here she is shown upon the *vāhana* Garuda and she holds a *śaṅkha* and *gadā* with two of her hands whereas one male and female attendant are present on either side in seated posture below the *pitha*.

A unique Vaiṣṇavī image is found in the Virattanesvara temple of Tiruttani. Here the deity is seated in the *ardhaparyaṅka* posture. The four-armed Vaiṣṇavī with *vāhana* Garuda beneath her seat is displayed with *cakra* and *śaṅkha* in her back hands while her front right hand is shown with *abhaya mudrā* and her front left hand rests on the lap. She is decorated with various ornaments like *makara-kuṇḍala*, *vājū-bandha*, beaded necklace and *mekhalā* on her loin. She wears a *kirīṭa-mukuṭa*. *Siraschakra* is noticed on the back of her head[12]. Artistically this sculpture may be assigned to the 12th century A.D. (Plate.6)

Another well designed Vaiṣṇavī is preserved in the Patna Museum of Bihar. The deity is seated in the *ardhaparyaṅka* āsana. The *vāhana* Garuḍa is placed beneath the seat. Her right hands are represented with a *cakra* and a vase or fruit which is not identified. Her back left hand is displayed with a *gadā* while her front left hands holds a baby. She wears *vājū-bandha*, anklets, *makara-kuṇḍala*, *mekhalā* and a beaded necklace which runs through her breasts. She is crowned with a decorative *kirīṭa-mukuṭa.* This image may be ascribed to the 12th century A.D on the basis of iconography. (Plate.7).

Depiction in Odishan Art

A beautiful specimen of the goddess Vaiṣṇavī is reported in the Paraśurāmeśvara temple of Bhubaneswar. Here the deity is seated in the *sattvaparyaṅka* posture. Her front hands are displayed with *vīja-pūraka* and a vessel. Her uplifted back hands are represented with *cakra* and conch[13]. Her hair is matted in a flat chignon on the top of her head. A *patra-kuṇḍala* hangs from each ear lobe. She wears *kūcha-bandha* and other decorative ornaments. The *vāhana* Garuda is not visible on the pedestal. This image may be assigned to the 7th century A.D.

Another Vaiṣṇavī image is found in the sanctum of the Vaital temple of Bhubaneswar. She is seated in the *vajraparyaṅka* pose. Her lower hands are projected with *vīja-pūraka* and conch while her uplifted hands are shown with mace and *cakra*. She wears a diadem at the base of her *kirīṭa-mukuṭa*. She is adorned with other ornaments like *makara-kuṇḍala*, *vājū-bandha*, hāra and *kaṭisūtra*. Garuda is placed on the right corner of the pedestal. This sculpture may be dated to the 8th century A.D. (Plate.8)

At Simhanatha the goddess Vaiṣṇavī is seated in *lalitāsana* with her front right hand in *varada*, the palm marked with a small lotus medallion, and her left hand holding a conch. Her uplifted hands hold the mace and *cakra*. Garuda is seated in *vajraparyaṅka* at the centre of the pedestal. In the Mātṛkā set in the compound of the Madhukesvara temple she is also seated in *lalitāsana* with her hands displaying *varada* and holding a conch. Her back hands hold a *cakra* and mace. At Shergarh she is seated in *lalitāsana* with her front hands showing *varada* and holding a vessel. Her uplifted back hands hold a conch and *cakra*. Her hair is matted on top of her head. The only notable changes on these early images is the elimination of the *vīja-pūraka*, being replaced by a small lotus mark on the palm, the gradual replacement of the vessel by a *śaṅkha* (conch), and the adoption of the *lalitāsana* pose.

In the Mātṛkā set at Paikapada, Vaiṣṇavī displays *abhaya* with her front right hand. Her uplifted back hands hold *cakra* and conch. Facial features coiffure, and pedestal are badly eroded. In the set on slab from Ranipur-Jharial she is seated in *ardhaparyaṅka* posture while cradling the child. Her back hands hold the conch and *cakra*. She wears a *kirīṭa-mukuṭa*. These images belong to 9th and 10th century A.D. A mutilated Vaiṣṇavī image is found in the Candi temple of Belkhandi, Here the deity is seated in the *ardhaparyaṅka* posture. The four-armed deity is represented with *śaṅkha* and *cakra* in her uplifted back hands. The lower two hands are broken from the elbow. She is place on double petalled lotus throne. Beneath the pedestal the *vāhana* Garuda is noticed. The goddess wears *kuṇḍala*, *hāra* and *kaṭisūtra* as decorative ornaments. She also wears a conical *kirīṭa-mukuṭa*. Two devotees with *añjalī-mudrā* are found on the either side of the bottom of the pedestal. This badly damaged image may be dated to the 10th century A.D. (Plate.9)

A unique image of Vaiṣṇavī is reported from the Dasasvamedha-ghat of Jajpur. This sculpture is artistically designed. Here the deity is seated in the *ardhaparyaṅka* posture. She is four-armed. Her uplifted hands are displayed with *śaṅkha* and *cakra* while her lower right hand is shown in *varada mudrā* and the left hand carries a child. She wears a jewellled diadem at the base of her gem-studded *kirīṭa-mukuṭa*, *a yañjopavīta*, beaded necklace, anklets, *vājū-bandha* and *kaṭisūtra* like decorative ornaments. Garuda looks up at her from the pedestal with his hands folded in *añjalī-mudrā*. This image is assigned to the 10th century A.D. (Plate.10).

In the Sathalapura Mātṛkā shrine another Vaiṣṇavī image is found. However the head of the deity is mutilated. She is seated in *ardhaparyaṅka* posture. The upper hands are broken. The lower right hand is projected with *varada mudrā* while the lower left hand carries a baby on her lap. The *vāhana* Garuda is noticed below on the pedestal. The goddess wears beaded necklace, *vājū-bandha, pāuji and kaṭisūtra* as decorative ornaments. This image may be ascribed to the 11th century A.D. (Plate.11)

Another four-armed Vaiṣṇavī is reported from Dharmasala of Jajpur. Here the deity is seated in the *ardhaparyaṅka* pose. The uplifted right hand is displayed with *cakra* while the corresponding hand is shown with *śaṅkha*. The lower right hand is broken from the elbow and the lower left hand carries a baby like the image of Sathalapura. She wears beaded necklace, ear-rings, *vājū-bandha*, anklets, *kaṭisūtra* and *yajñopavīta*. Besides, she wears a conical *kirīṭa-mukuṭa* having a diadem. In the image a *makara-toraṇa* frames the head of Vaiṣṇavī. Garuda with *añjalī-mudrā* is placed below on the pedestal. This image may be dated to the 11th century A.D. (Plate.12)

It is to be noted that in these Mātṛkā images of Vaiṣṇavī, the *cakra* and the conch are the *āyudhas* most closely associated with her. The mace appears on only a few early images prior to the introduction of a child. In the battle frieze on the Somesvara temple at Mukhalingam, in contrast, the two-armed Vaiṣṇavī attacks the *asura* with a mace held in her raised right hand. In the martial set of Mātṛkā images in the Samalai temple at Sonepur, the mace is held in her principal right hand while the conch is in her corresponding left hand. Her uplifted back hands hold a *cakra* and a lotus (?). She is depicted in a frontal pose seated on the shoulders of the kneeling Garuda. She wears a long *muṇḍamāla*. A small dancing female attendant holding a mace and a sword accompanies her on the left[14].

A beautiful specimen of Vaiṣṇavī image is reported from Khiching of Mayurbhanja. Here the goddess is seated in the *ardhaparyaṅka* posture. She is four-armed and her upper right hand is displayed with *cakra* while her corresponding left hand is shown with *śaṅkha*. The lower right hand is projected with *abhaya mudrā* and the lower left hand carries a baby. She wears designed necklace, *vājū-bandha*, bangles, anklets, *pauji, kaṭisūtra, yajñopavīta* and *makara-kuṇḍala* as ear-rings. Moreover, she is adorned with a conical *kirīṭa mukuṭa*. Garuda with *añjalī-mudrā* is found beneath the seat on the pedestal. The flying *vidyādharas* are noticed on the either side of the upper stone slab. This image may be ascribed to the 11th century A.D. (Plate.13)

An image of Vaiṣṇavī is noticed on the upper story of the Daksaprajapati Śiva temple at Banapur. She is seated in *lalitāsana* on a *viśvapadma* and is four-armed. Her front hands show *varada* and rest on a mace while her uplifted back hands hold the *cakra* and conch. Her face is obliterated but her tall *kirīṭa-mukuṭa* is visible. She duplicates the pose and iconography of Viṣṇu except the *āyudhas* in the uplifted hands are reversed and Garuda is not beneath her seat. Similar Vaiṣṇavī images are housed in the upper *rāhā* niches in the syncretistic iconographical programme of the temple. In each case the Devī is standing in a rigid frontal pose and is flanked on either side by a female attendant. The Devī has her front set of hands lowered while her back set is uplifted. On the north and south sides the images are nearly identical except for the manner in which the sword is held. The lowered hands hold a *cakra* and rest on the mace. The back right hand holds the sword, either upright with the hand held at the waist or raised horizontally above her head, while the left hand holds a conch. On the west side the front right hand, now broken off, presumably held arrows while the left hand has a bow. The uplifted hands hold a lotus and a *cakra*. The image is similar to one in an upper story *pāga* niche on the Magheśvara temple at Bhubaneswar, except a *cakra* replaces the sword and she stands on the back of a lion.

In the sanctum of the Nārāyaṇī temple of village Dia in the District of Khordha a Vaiṣṇavī image is found. She is worshipped by the local people under the name Nārāyaṇī. Here the deity is four-armed. She is seated in the *vajraparyaṅka* posture. Her upper right hand is displayed with *cakra* while the corresponding left hand is shown with *śaṅkha*. The lower right and left hands are projected with *varada* and *abhaya Mudrā* respectively. Except for the transposed *āyudhas* in the back hands, the iconography relates to the descriptions of the *Mayamata*[15]. She wears the decorative ornaments like necklace, bangles, long *vanamāla* along with a *kirīṭa mukuṭa* which adorns her head. The *vāhana* Garuda appears at the center of the pedestal. Her head is framed by a *makara-toraṇa* motif as described in the book *Khākharā Temples*[16]. This image may be assigned to the 14th century A.D. (Plate.14)

In the martial set of Mātṛkā images in the Samalai temple at Sonepur, the goddess Vaiṣṇavī is found seated on the shoulders of kneeling Garuda. Here the mace is held in her principal right hand while the conch is in her corresponding left hand. Her uplifted back hands hold a *cakra* and an object which is obscure. She is decorated with *makara- kuṇḍala*, necklace and other normal ornaments; she is crowned with a *kirīṭa-mukuṭa.* She wears a long *muṇḍa-māla* as described by T E.Donaldson. A small dancing female attendant holding a mace and a sword accompanies her on the lower left corner of the stone slab. This image may be ascribed to the 18th century A.D.(Plate.15)

Thus, these are the prominent Vaiṣṇavī sculptures found elsewhere of India which shed light on the art and iconographic features of the Vaiṣṇavī images. The sculptural representation of the cited images will definitely glorify the cultural as well as the art history of our sub-continent.

Table 2: Table showing the location and period of Vaiṣṇavī images of India

Deity	Place	Museum	Period
Vaiṣṇavī	Alampur, Mahabubnagar	Alampur Museum Mahabubnagar (A.P.)	7th cent. A.D.
Vaiṣṇavī	Devagana Rajasthan	Baroda Museum (Gujarat)	8th cent. A.D.
Vaiṣṇavī	Amjhera (Rajasthan)	Baroda Museum (Gujarat)	8th cent. A.D.
Vaiṣṇavī	Chezerla (Guntur A.P)		8th cent. A.D.
Vaiṣṇavī	Tiruchatturai (Tanjaur, Madras)		9th cent. A.D.
Vaiṣṇavī	Khajuraho (Chhatarpur)	Archaeological Museum Khajuraho	9th cent. A.D.
Vaiṣṇavī		Archaeological Museum, Bhopal	9th cent. A.D.
Vaiṣṇavī		Central Museum, Indore	9th cent. A.D.
Vaiṣṇavī		Central Museum Gwalior	9th cent. A.D.
Vaiṣṇavī		District Museum, Rajgarh	10th cent. A.D.
Vaiṣṇavī		Dr. H.S. Gaur Museum, Sagar	10th cent. A.D.
Vaiṣṇavī	Lanji (Balaghat)	A.S.I. Collection at Langi, Balaghat	10th cent. A.D.
Vaiṣṇavī	Ashapuri (Raisen)	Birla Museum, Bhopal	10th cent. A.D.
Vaiṣṇavī	Chausatha Yogini Temple at Bheraghat Jabalpur		10th cent. A.D.
Vaiṣṇavī	Baijnath Almora	Museum at Baijnath Almora	10th cent. A.D.
Vaiṣṇavī		Bharat Kala Bhawan, Varanasi	10th cent. A.D.
Vaiṣṇavī	Siron Lalitpur, (U.P.)		11th cent. A.D.
Vaiṣṇavī	Hinglajgarh (Mandsaur)	Central Museum, Indore	11th cent. A.D.

Vaiṣṇavī		Patna Museum, Patna, Bihar	12th cent. A.D.
Vaiṣṇavī	Lanji (Balaghat)	A.S.I. Collection Lanji (Balaghat)	12th cent. A.D.
Vaiṣṇavī	Tiruttani, Virattanesvara temple		12th cent. A.D.
Vaiṣṇavī		Central Archaeological Museum, Gwalior	12th cent. A.D.

Table 3: Table Showing the location, attributes and period of Vaiṣṇavī images of Odisha

Place	Attributes	Pose	Period
Bhub:Parasuramesvara	vīja-pūraka, cakra, conch, vessel	sattvaparyaṅka	7th cent. A.D.
Bhub:Vaital Deul	vīja-pūraka, mace, cakra, conch	vajraparyaṅka	8th cent. A.D.
Simhanatha Island	varada, mace, cakra, conch	lalitāsana	9th cent. A.D.
Muk:Madhukesvara	Varada, cakra, mace, conch	lalitāsana	9th cent. A.D.
Shergh:Durga Temple	varada, conch, cakra, vessel	lalitāsana	9th cent. A.D.
Paikapada:Patalesvara	abhaya, cakra, conch, child	lalitāsana	9th cent. A.D.
Ranipur-Jharial	abhaya, conch, cakra, child	ardhaparyaṅka	9th cent. A.D.
Belkhandi:Candi	abhaya, cakra conch, child	lalitāsana	10th cent. A.D.
Puri:Markandeya tank	child	lalitāsana	10th cent. A.D.
Jip:Dasasvamedha-ghat	abhaya, cakra conch, child	lalitāsana	10th cent. A.D.
Khicing	abhaya, cakra conch, child	lalitāsana	10th cent. A.D.

Pedagadi:Bhimesvari	child	lalitāsana	10th cent. A.D.
Sathalapura	abhaya, child	lalitāsana	10th cent. A.D.
Dharmasala(OSM)	abhaya, cakra conch, child	lalitiāsana	11th cent. A.D.
Salepur Museum	abhaya, cakra conch, child	lalitāsana	11th cent. A.D.
Garedipancana	abhaya, cakra conch, child	lalitāsana	11th cent. A.D.
Banpur:Daksaprajapati	varada, cakra conch, mace	lalitāsana	13th cent. A.D.
Dia:Daksina Kali	varada, cakra, conch, abhaya	vajraparyaṅka	14th cent. A.D.
Madhupugarh: Jagannatha	varada, cakra conch, abhaya	vajraparyaṅka	15th cent. A.D.
Sonepur:Samalai	mace, cakra, conch	garudāsana	18th cent., A.D.

References

1. R.C. Agrawala, *Sculptures from South Western Rajasthan*, p.70.
2. Photo *A.I.I.S.* No. 194.9713, Varanasi.
3. *Ibid.*
4. Bajpai, K. D., *Catalogue of Devi Gallery*, Birla Museum, Bhopal, p.9, pl.8.
5. O.P. Misra, *Iconography of the Saptamātṛkā*, Delhi, 1989, p.82.
6. R.K., Shrama, *The Chaushtha Yogini Temple at Bheraghat*, Delhi, 1978, p.146.
7. S.B. Singh, *Brahmanical Icons in Northern India*, Delhi, 1977, p.167.
8. Based on information given by Dr. S.D. Trivedi, Director, State Museum, Lucknow.
9. R.S., Garg, Śākta *Pratimayen* (Hindi) Murtikala Vol.II, Central Museum, Indore, Bhopal,1980, p.54.
10. Based on photo from *A.I.I.S.* Varanasi.

11. *op.cit*, p.32.
12. D.R.Rajeshweri, *Iconography of* Śakti, New Delhi, 1989, p.44.
13. T Donaldson, *Hindu Temple Art of Orissa*, Vol. III, Leiden, 1985-87 fig. 3279.
14. T E. Donaldson, *Tantra and* Śākta *Art of Orissa*, Vol.I, New Delhi, 2002, P.346.
15. T E.Donaldson, *op.cit*, P.347
16. Sanjaya Kumar Mahapatra, *Khākharā Temples*, Delhi, 2016, P.72.

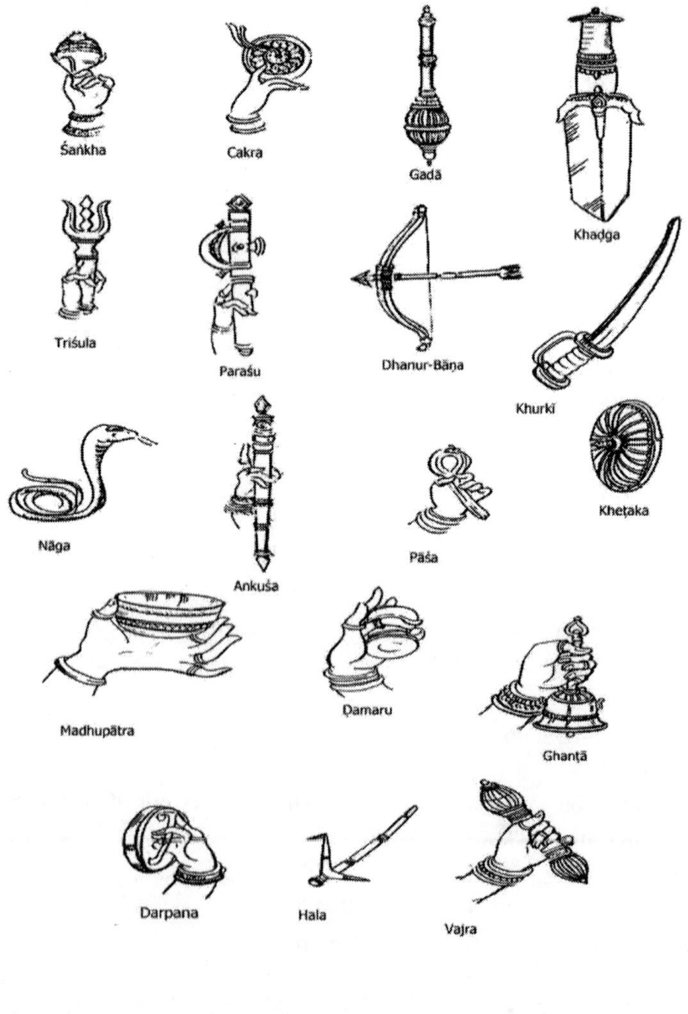

6

RITUALS

The celebration of rituals and cult practices associated with the religious festivals usually reflect the culture of the people in a telescopic form. The observances like *vrata*, *pūjā*, *utsava* along with the music and dance keep the traditional system continuing, binding the community in a socio-cultural fabric. Above all, the performance of a particular festival is the parameter of a society.

Hindu religious festivals are numerous in Orissa ranging from the tribal and semi-tribal communities to the people of the advanced and sophisticated society. Some of them are of national importance, some are widespread irrespective of caste and creed, and some others are confined to particular communities. Generally, most of them are religious in nature and are linked with the propitiation of some gods or goddesses. However, these festivals are observed in a ritualistic manner in Orissa and some of them are the off springs of the cult practices prevailing in the sacred shrines. That is why it is very important to study the rituals and cult practices which ultimately lead to the emergence of festivals. The ritualistic observances associated with the cult of Mother Goddess are recorded here which will throw light on the widespread prevalence of Saktism in Orissa. Besides, the ritualistic pattern and practices involved in the worship of the goddess will certainly keep the cult tradition alive providing solace, enjoyment and moral strength to the participants which will ultimately pave the way for the spiritual upliftment.

RITUAL AND ITS UTILITY

Ritual is an art, the art of religion. While art is the outward material expression of ideas intellectually held and emotionally felt, the ritual art on the other hand is the expression of those ideas and feeling which are specifically called religious[1]. It is the mode by which religious truth is presented, and made intelligible in material forms and symbols to the mind. It appeals to all natures passionately, sensible of that beauty in which, to some, God must manifest himself. But it is more than this. For, it is the means by which the mind is transformed and purified. According to Indian principles it is the instrument whereby the consciousness of the worshipper (Sādhaka) is shaped in actual fact into forms of experience containing the truths which scriptures teach[2]. In broad conception ritual and cult practices are inter-related and used synonymously. But in this chapter both the terms have been employed differently. While ritual is used for the normal pūjā, the cult practices are applied for the special ritualistic patterns adopted during the time of special occasions such as Śāradiya Durgā pūjā and *Vāsantika Durgā pūjā*. While discussing the ritualistic aspect of the goddess we have to bear in the mind that it is of purital style. The worship consists of *pūjā*, donations, sacrifices, *vratas*, meditation and pilgrimage to Śākta Pīṭhas[3]. The *pūjā* is generally performed by the individuals[4] and by the community. *Durgāpūjā* in the *Navarātra* and *RathaYātrā* are the examples where large functions are arranged to perform community *pūjā*. For an individual *Sādhaka*, the *Purāṇas* specifically prescribe the codes of *sadācāra*. It is said that a man devoid of good character is always a failure in this world and afterwards[5].

Even much importance has been given to the Śākta Brāhmins in the *Devī Bhāgavata Purāṇa* in respect of the performance of the rites and sacrifice based on the Vedic mantras. However, in the *Devī Purāṇa* it has been mentioned that everybody should worship the goddess for the happiness in life[6] and for the attainment of *caturvargaphalaprāpti* such as *dharma*, *artha*, *kāma* and *mokṣa*.

Adhikārī

The worship of Durgā Mahiṣāsuramardinī, Mātṛkās and other female divinities is very much cosmopolitan in nature and it is performed not only by Brāhmins but also by those who are outside the pale of the caste system[7]. She is worshipped by the various groups of *mlechhas*, by the *dasyus*, by the people from Aṅga, Baṅga and Kaliṅga countries and by the *kinnaras*, barbars and Śakas[8]. Only one condition is there, that the devotees should be full of devotion, should have to take bath and should be cheerful and jolly[9].

THE WORSHIP PROCEDURE

During the worship of the Divine Mothers certain ritualistic procedures is adopted by the priests. The related methods of performance are furnished below for reference.

The Medium of Worship

By the study of the *Purāṇas*, it is known that the goddess is generally worshipped by the people on the river banks by constructing clay images. However, the *Kālīkā Purāṇa* states that the medium of worship of the different goddesses are usually *pratimā* (image in a temple), *maṇḍala*, *yantra*, *liṅga*, *ghaṭa* (pot), *khaḍga*, and *citra*[10]. A newly constructed image is to be infused with life (*pratiṣṭhā*) to confer divinity on it[11].

Yoginī-Tantra says that the Devī should be worshipped either in *pratimā, maṇḍala* or *yantra.*

Places of Worship

The best place of worship are the holy places, river-sides, caves, *tirthas*, summits of mountains, confluences of rivers, holy forests, foot of bel tree, temples of Śiva and even the body of the worshipper. In order to be more effective the female deity should be worshipped in the Śākta Pīṭhas as described by *Devī Purāṇa* and *Kālīkā Purāṇa*. The image of the Devī may be worshipped in the houses as well.

Time for Worship

According to the *Nigama Kalpataru*, the daily worship should begin after the passing of the half of the first *prahara* and finished at the end of the ten *daṇḍas* (*ghaṭis*).i.e. one and a half hours after the sun-rise and before expiry of four hours[12]. The *Devī Bhāgavata Purāṇa* describes that mother goddesses are to be worshipped at a time when the sun remains in the *Kanyā-rāśi*[13]. Apart from the *navarātra*, she should be worshipped in the eighth or fourteenth day of the dark fortnight (*aṣṭamyāṁvāchaturdaśyāṁ*) as per the description of the *Devī Mahātmya*. The days preferred for worship are Tuesday and Saturday.

Seats and Postures

According to the *Sādhanā Rahasya*, *japa, pūjā, dhyāna* and so forth should be performed sitting in postures such as *padmāsana, ardhāsana*, *sukhāsana, siddhāsana* etc. Otherwise the pūjā will be ineffectual. Even these āsanas are helpful for concentration, *samādhi* and for full absorption in the divinity.

Rosaries

Rosaries made of beads of *rudrākṣa*, conch-shell, lotus-seed, wild-olive, pearls, crystals, gems, gold, coral, silver, turmeric, sandal, tulsi, roots of *kusha* grass are prescribed for worship. Preferably *rudrākṣa* and red-sandal beads are used for the Devī worship.

Purification

Purification of the 'Five' (*pañca śuddhi*) has been prescribed in the *Kulārṇava* *Tantra* (VI *ullāsa* VV.16-22). Before the worship of the goddess, it is very essential to purify the 'Five' such as purification of self (*ātmaśuddhi*), of place (*ṣṭhāna śuddhi*), of mantra (*mantra śuddhi*), of articles for worship (*dravya śuddhi*), and of *devatā* (*devatā śuddhi*). These are also described in the *pūjā-paddhati* (worship-procedure).

Articles used in Worship

There are sixteen *upacharās* or articles used in the worship of Mahiṣāsuramardinī or any female divinity. These *upacharās* are 1.*āsana* (seat of the image); 2.*svāgata* (welcome); 3.*pādya* (water for washing the feet); 4.*arghya* (offering of water mixed with flowers, unboiled white rice, sandal paste etc); 5.*ācamana* (water for sipping and cleansing the lips); 6.*madhuparka* (honey, ghee, milk and curd offered in a silver or brass vessel); 7.*punarācamana* (water for sipping for the second time); 8.*snāna* (water for bathing); 9.*vasana* (cloth); 10. *ābharaṇa* (Jewells); 11.*gandha* (perfume and sandal paste); 12.*puṣpa* (flowers); 13.*dhūpa* (incense); 14.*dīpa* (light); 15.*naivedya* (food); 16.*vandana* or *namaskāra* (prayer). The *Purāṇas* enlist the following things to be used in her worship and offered in *naivedya*, such as water, milk, bel-leaf, ghee, red- flowers, *tila*, sugar, red-lotuses, red-clothes, *ghanṭā*, *cāmara*, ornaments and all other things offered to her with devotion and śraddhā[14].

Donations

Each and everything obtained in right way may be donated in honour of Devī. Even vegetables and non-vegetables may be offered in donation to virgin girls or ladies, Brāhmins or devotees of Devī[15], and goddess is highly pleased by such donations. The donated articles are like land, gold, cows, paddy, *tila*, clothes and ghee etc. things of necessity of life[16].

Agnisthāpana or Homa

Maintenance of the sacred fire or *homa* is a duty of those who are well-versed in the literatures of the *vāmacāra*, the *dakṣiṇācāra* as well as in *vedāntācāra*. As homa is a part and parcel of *pañcāṅga karma*, it should be performed with devotion. It is believed that gods or goddesses reside in the sacred fire so it is the pious duty of a devotee to perform *homa* at the end of the *pūjā* ritual. The *Devī Purāṇa* states that the performance of *homa* is permitted to the higher castes as well as to śūdras, woman and children[17]. However, Brahmin ritualists are employed in Orissa for the performance of *homa* and *yajña*. *Homa* or *yajña* is the making of offering to fire. Generally pure ghee with a wooden spoon is poured into the fire-pit (*kuṇḍa*) chanting the mantra of the desired deity.

WORSHIP OF DIVINITY

The individual worship is conceived as a complex and an elaborate art in Hinduism. Worship through the medium of symbols, images or *yantras* are intended to supplement the efforts towards God realization. As such, *pratīkopāsanā* or symbolical worship is essential for an aspirant for divinization.

Types of Worship

The worship of gods or goddesses is of threefold character viz. *sātvika* worship, consisting of *japa* and offering of vegetarian *naivedya*, *rājasi* worship is effected by *bali*, and offering of *naivedya* containing meat, and *tāmasika* worship is performed by the offerings of wine, meat etc. Besides, at a number of places, the *Devī Bhāgavata* has mentioned two types of worship i.e. internal and external. The external one is again of two types such as *vaidikī* and *tāntrikī* while internal form of worship emphasizes on the pure, attributeless form of goddess, the external form of worship gives stress on the exterior objects[18]. In Orissa apart from the above cited types of worship, another type of worship is noticed which is called *miśra* i.e. the combination of *vaidikī* and *tāntrikī*. However, in the seventh chapter of the *Gautamīya Tantra* it is mentioned that "worship is of five kinds, namely *abhigamana*, *upādāna*, Ijyā, *svādhyāya* and yoga". *Abhigamana* is a custom for cleansing the place of worship and removing the pastes, flowers and garlands etc. from the image. *Upādāna* is the collection of materials for worship. *Ijyā* is a term applied for the worship of *Iṣṭadevatā* as per the proper procedure prescribed in the *śāstras*. *Svādhyāya* is the doing of japa and recitation of hymns. Yoga is the mediation of *Iṣṭadevatā* in one's mind for self absorption. The deity is also worshipped in the subtle form, in gross form and in the combination of both the forms corresponding to the *parā*, *aparā* and *parāparā* worship-methods of the *śāstras*.

Preliminary Rites before Worship

Certain preliminary rites are preformed before the commencement of pūjā rites. The worshipper or the ritualist after rising in the morning performs daily morning duties including oblation and *sandhyā*. Then worshipping the deities at the doors of the temple shrine, he enters into the *pūjāgriha* where the image is installed. Thereafter the seat (*āsana*), the offering materials are purified. Salutation is offered to the Guru, Ganapati, Durgā, Brahmā and Ananta for support. The obstructive spirits are driven away (*bhūtāpasāraṇa*) and the ten quarters are fenced from their attack by striking the earth three times with the left foot uttering the weapon-mantra (*astra-vīja*) "*phat*" and by snapping the fingers round the head. Besides, the offering of *upacāra*, other rituals such as *prāṇayāma* (breath-control) *bhūtaśuddhi, nyāsa, dhyāna, praṇāma* (obeisance) etc, are performed. The object of *bhūtaśuddhi* is the removal of evils and the purification of the elements of which body is composed[19]. The *Mantramahodadhi* speaks that it is a rite which is preliminary to the worship of a god or goddess. By this ritual a mental process of evolution takes place where the body is in thought resolved into the source from where it has come[20]. The object of *nyāsa* is to make the body spiritualized. This is the process through which the sinful body of *Sādhaka* or worshipper is dissolved and infused with the life of divinity. Hence, the ritual methods like *prāṇayāma, dhyāna, japa, nyāsa* etc are very essential to withdraw the mind from the external attraction and repulsions in order to concentrate it on the deity worshipped.

Puraścaraṇa

Puraścaraṇa is indispensable for every aspirant to achieve success in the path of God-realization. *Puraścaraṇa* is a term applied for the attainment of *siddhi* (success) through a definite procedure consisting of five parts such as *japa* (repeated utterance of mantra according to certain rules), *homa* (sacred fire sacrifice) *tarpaṇa* (satisfying the deity with water), *mārjjana* (sprinkling of water) and *Brāhmaṇa bhojana* (feasting of Brāhmins). It may be noted that the sacrificial pits (*kuṇḍas*) are of different shapes according to the object desired to be achieved. The above described ritualistic rules are applied for the worship of all the divine beings. Moreover, on the basis of ritualistic pattern the worship of the goddess may be categorized under two broad heads as daily worship (*nitya pūjā*) and occasional worship (*naimitika pūjā*). The occasional worship includes the śāradiya navarātra and *vāsantika navarātra* which is meant for the special worship with utmost devotion. However, there are certain basic principles which are normally applied both for the daily worship and occasional worship. Both the patterns of worship are based on the sources available in the palm-leaf manuscripts specially found in our land.

The aims and objectives of the rituals are far-reaching. By the practice of the worship procedure the aspirant feels that he lives as close as possible to the Divinity in a mood of Holy Communion. Gradually the ritualistic performance leads the devotee or aspirant towards divinization so that the *Sādhaka* feels his identity with the Absolute which is the real goal of human life.

References

1. Mohanlal Bhagwandas Jhavery, *Comparative and Critical Study of Mantraśāstra,* Ahmedabad, 1944, p. 47.
2. *Ibid.*
3. *Devī Bhāgavata Purāṇa*, p. XI. 8-13; XI. 16. 15-16.
4. *Ibid.* XI. 16. 17; 6.
5. *Ibid.* XI. 23.24-28.
6. *Devī Purāṇa*p.22.5; 23.3-5.
7. *Ibid.* p.89.19.
8. *Ibid.* p.88.1-3.
9. *Ibid.* p.22.6-7.
10. *Kālīkā Purāṇa*, p.59. 185-186; 60. 21-32.
11. *Ibid.*, 83. 2-3
12. As Quoted By Mohanlal Bhagwandes Jhavery, *op.cit*, p.75.
13. *Devī Bhāgavata Purāṇa*, VII, 117. 7-9; 124. 1-2.
14. *Kālīkā Purāṇa*, p. 59. 161.

15. *Devī purāṇa*, p. 102. 3-4.
16. *Ibid.*, p.109. 7-8
17. Ibid., p. 121.1-32
18. P. G. Lalye, Studies on Devī Bhāgavata, Bombay, 1973 p.196.
19. Monier William, Sanskrit-English Dictionary, New Delhi, 2008, p.742.
20. John Woodroffe, *Introduction to Tantra Śāstra*, Madras, 1990, p.109.

7

CONCLUSION

The Mātṛkā worship plays a vital role in the cultural as well as sculptural history of India. Although the worship of Divine Mother owes its genesis to a hoary past yet the appearance of the Mātṛkā worship was wide spread in our sub-continent during the Kushāṇa period and it became popular in Odisha during the period of Somavaṁśī reign. Generally the Mātṛkā deities receive offerings from the devotees in a set or group under the name Saptamātṛkā or Aṣṭamātṛkā but individual images of Cāmuṇḍā and Vārāhī are worshipped by the people for which separate temples were also built by the kings and feudal lords. The present context regards the Mātṛkās as the Śakti embodiments of respective gods on the basis of the descriptions of the Brahmanical literature, who in iconic sculptural portrayals are the divine mothers and warriors, used for ritual worship. To add more, Mātṛkā worship and the related manifestations in plastic arts are a pan-Indian phenomenon, the antiquity of which is considered to be as ancient as that of Śiva and fertility goddesses of the Indus valley civilization

The history of mother goddess or Mātṛkā is as old as civilization. E. Mackay traces the worship of Saptamātṛkās in India back to third millennium B.C. A famous seal recovered from the Indus valley to 2000 years before the Christian Era, represents, indeed, an arboreal female deity standing between the wide apart branches of a Pipal tree while seven human figures, representing in all probability as many female deities or spirits or attendants as indicated by the long plait of hair being displayed by each of them, are depicted her in a row. These seven female figures, as admitted that they do represent deities, may have, been the `ancestress' of Saptamātṛkās, the seven divine mothers found in the later Hindu, Buddhist and Jaina pantheons. However in India the figure seven has always had a character of special sacredness, being employed to express an indefinite plurality of sacred objects as in the causes of the seven partitions of the worlds, seven holy cities, the seven holy rivers, seven seers and so on. In the Śakti context, besides being conventionally the number of the divine mothers or Mātṛkās, seven is also the number of the deified flaming tongues of Agni, mentioned in Vedic and Upanishad literature as the seven 'Red Sisters'

Saptamātṛkās or the seven mothers represent the endowed energies of the important familiar Male deities. They are *Brahmāṇī* (Sarasvatī), Māheśvarī (Raudrī), Kaumārī (Kārttikeyāṇī), Vaiṣṇavī (Lakṣmī), Vārāhī, Indrāṇī (Mahendri) and Cāmuṇḍā (Cāmuṇḍī). There are, however, occasional variations in the list of the Mātṛkās with regard to their number and the order of their enumeration; usually they are seven, though eight or more of them can be counted in some cases. In the epic like the *Mahābhārata* we get references about a group of goddesses collectively known as Mātṛkās, appearing in a series of episodes, in which they are mainly associated with Skanda Kārttikeya as their allies. Their physical descriptions emphasize their fearsome natures, and their behaviour is constantly said to be violent.

The *Skanda Purāṇa*, the *Devī Purāṇa* and the *Brahmavaivarta Purāṇa* mention more Mātṛkās where as only eight Mātṛkās have been mentioned by the *Devībhāgabata Purāṇa*, the *Nityaṣoḍaśikārṇava*, the *Prapañchasāra Tantra*, the *Liṅga Purāṇa*, the *Mantramahodadhi* and the *Varāha Purāṇa*.

Regarding the origin of the Mātṛkās, there are two different puranic versions. According to the *Mārkaṇḍeya Purāṇa* the Mātṛkās aided Ambika along with Cāmuṇḍā in causing death of the most powerful ally of the demon king Śumbha named Raktabīrja.

The iconographical feature of these Saptamātṛkās are recorded in details in the *Agni Purāṇa*, the *Aṁśumadbhedāgama* the *Pūrvakaraṇāgama*, the *Matsya Purāṇa*, the *Rūpāvatāra*, Ś*ilparatnakoṣa* and *Viśvakarmāśāstra*. Gopinatha Rao has given more details regarding the iconography of the seven mothers in his work on Hindu iconography as these are the female counterparts who are armed with the same weapons, wear the same ornaments and ride the same *vāhanas* and carry the same banners, as their corresponding male gods do. The *Mārkaṇḍeya Purāṇa* refers that the Śaktis of the individual gods are characterized by the respective forms, ornaments and mounts of those gods.

It means *Brahmāṇī* should be sculptured like *Brahmā*, Māheśvarī like Maheśvara, Vaiṣṇavī like Viṣṇu, Vārāhī as a short woman with an angry face and bearings a plough as her weapon, Indrāṇī like Indra; and Cāmuṇḍā as a terrific woman. This last goddess should have her hair in a disheveled condition, should one of her hands and carry a *kapāla* in another. All the Mātṛkās are to be seated images and they should have two of their hands held in the *varada* and *abhaya* poses while the other two hands should carry weapons appropriate with the male counterparts of the female powers. They are shown seated upon either *padmāsana* or *ardhaparyaṅka* posture in the sculptures.

According to the *Varāha Purāṇa*, the Mātṛkās are the eight mother goddesses who represent eight mental qualities like

- Yogeśvarī represents *Kāma* or desire
- Māheśvarī, *krodha* or anger
- Vaiṣṇavī, *lobha* or covetousness
- Brāhmanī, *mada* or pride
- Kaumārī, *moha* or illusion
- Indrāṇī, *matsarya* or faultfinding, jealousy
- Cāmuṇḍā, *paisunya* or animal passion
- Vārāhī, *asuya* or hatredness

Odisha, being a great center of Saktism, exhibits all manifestations of Śakti in the temple arts as well as in literatures. Through this Mātṛkā cult is believed to have been prevailing in the region from a very ancient past, it is only from sixth or seventh century on words that definite historical evidence are found. The worship of Saptamātṛkā as an important manifestation of Śakti, was wide spared throughout Odisha with images appearing as early as the seventh century. But royal patronage was especially given in the tenth century i.e. at the end of the Bhauma period and the beginning of the Somavaṁśī period as may be observed some of the images, as at jajpur, are monumental in size.

The Trantric form of Saktism centering round the cult of Saptamātṛkās, however, seems to have reached the climax when the temple of Vaital (Odisha) was built in or about A.D. 8th/9th century during the rule of Bhauma karas. It is worthy to note that during this period Saivism, Saktism and Tantricism seem to have been inseparably mixed up and formed a strange amalgam.

The goddess Vaiṣṇavī, one of the benign aspects of the Divine Mother, has been described both as a Mātṛkā and Yogini in the Indian literature. She is invariably displayed in the Saptamātṛkā panels hailing from various archaeological sites of India. It is to be noted that the sculptors of our land have presented the Vaiṣṇavī images starting from four-armed to the variety of six-armed. On the basis of their iconographical features the images of Saptamātṛkās can be divided into two groups. The earlier group does not hold babies in their arms, but the babies are invariably found in the arms or laps of the later Mātṛkās.

Iconolatry is not an ignorant or useless practice meant only for spiritual aspirants rather it serves as an ingredient to the human needs. The image-worship and associated ceremonial observances are certainly of immense value for spiritual advancement and material progress of mankind. It may be emphatically stated that both the worldly pleasures and the bliss of communion with Divinity are equally at the disposal of those who worship the goddess in any of her manifestations. Thus it is ascertained from the above accounts that the Divine Mother in her Vaiṣṇavī aspect has occupied a very significant place in the art-iconographic as well as in the socio-religious life of Odishan people in particular and of Indian people in general. The abundant archaeological remains, numerous myths associated with her miraculous power and her profuse representation in the art bespeak her hoary antiquity and wide celebrity as the Universal Mother.

GLOSSARY

Abhaṅga	:	A form of standing pose in which the plumb line or the centre line, from the crown of the head to a point midway between the heels, passes slightly to the right of the naval.
Ābharaṇa	:	Jewells.
Abhayā	:	Fearlessness.
Abhayāhasta		Hand pose, indicative of protection symbolising a deity's power to dispel fear.
abhayā- mudrā	:	Protective-pose in which the hand is raised with the palm outward and fingers stretched.
Ādarśa	:	Mirror.
Ādi - Śakti / Ādyā-Śakti	:	Primordial energy (mother goddess).
Āgamas	:	Sacred texts based on Tantricism.
Agni	:	Fire.
Akṣamālā	:	Rosary of beads

Āliḍha	:	A particular attitude where the right knee advanced and the left leg drawn back, it denotes a particular pose of standing in which the right knee is thrown to the front, the leg retracted and the left leg is diagonally stretched behind. Pratyāliḍha is just its opposite.
Añjali	:	Folded hands in prayer symbolizing reverence to a deity.
Ankuśa	:	Elephant goad.
Antarīya	:	Unstitched cloth wrapped around the waist and legs of a male person.
Anuratha	:	Narrow vertical recess separating pāgas.
Arcā	:	An image or idol destined to be worshipped.
Ardhaparyaṅka	:	Seated pose with one leg kept horizontally on the seat while the other knee is raised; in dance attitude one leg, folded, is kept horizontally and other is straight.
Ardhāsana	:	A seating posture.
Āsana	:	Seat; pedestal; a seated posture.
Asi	:	Sword.
Aṣṭabhūjā	:	Eight-armed goddess.
Aṣṭa- Caṇḍī pīṭhas	:	Eight prominent centers of Devī worship.
Aṣṭadikpālas	:	Guardians of eight (four cardinal and four intermediate) quarters.
Aṣṭmātṛkā	:	The eight mothers.

Aṣṭa- Kilā	:	eight prominent centers /seats of Devī worship in Odisha.
Asura	:	demon; opponent of the gods.
Āvaraṇa- devatā	:	Secondary deities surrounding the main presiding deity of the temple, forming a protective ring; they usually occupy the anuratha niches.
Āyudha	:	Symbolical weapon or attribute in the hands of a divinity.
Bali	:	Sacrifice of animal, white gourd and other objects before the gods and goddesses for their propitiation.
Balidāna	:	offering of animal-sacrifice as well as blood, meet, liquor etc.
Bāṇa	:	arrow.
Berā	:	an icon meant for worship.
Bhusuṇḍi	:	sling.
Bīju	:	rows of beads on upper arms.
Cakra	:	Wheel or Disc; the wheel of Viṣṇu, nerve plexuses within the body.
Cāmara	:	Fly-whisk or fan made with the tail of a yak.
Carma	:	Hide, shiled
Caṇḍīkā	:	a name of goddess Durgā.
Catuspīṭha	:	Four-pīṭhas or centers of worship.
Caurī	:	Fly-whisk.
Chhatrakam	:	Parasol or umbrella.
Churikā	:	knife.
carcīkā	:	Name of Cāmuṇḍā hand pose with a hand placed near the chin and the little finger, wet with blood, put into the mouth.

chinnamastaka	:	Severed human head
Cūḍāmaṇi	:	A kind of ornament bedecked with gem.
Ḍamaru	:	The drum of load Śiva, shaped like an hourglass.
Daṇḍa	:	A daṇḍais twenty four minutes; staff, stick, club.
Daśabhūjā	:	Ten-armed deity.
Daśamudrā	:	Ten kinds of postures like avāhana, Samsthāpana, Sannidhāna, Sannirodhana, Abaguṇṭhana etc.
Deula	:	General name for a Kaliṅgān temple.
Devī	:	Goddess
Dhanu	:	Bow.
Dhvajā	:	Banner, flag.
Gadā	:	Mace, club.
gaṇa	:	The group of spirits & denim-gods
Ghanṭa	:	a musical instrument.
Ghanṭā	:	Bell.
Hāra	:	long pearl necklace.
Hasta	:	arm, hand.
Jagamohana	:	Rectangular or square hall fronting the sanctum.
Jaṅghā	:	a vertical portion of the bāda between the pābhāga and the barāndā.
Jaṭā- Mukuṭa	:	a coil of matted and clotted hair forming a conical crown.
Kaliṅgān	:	of Kaliṅga or pertaining to Kaliṅga.
Kāñchi	:	a type of girdle (especially for goddess Kali).

Kaṅgan	:	Bracelet of beads.
kaṅkāla-mūrti		Skeletal figure of Tāntric deity.
Karṇika	:	Ear-rings of trumpet shape.
Kanthā	:	a short necklace of beads with central pendant and looped chain.
Kapāla	:	Bowl made with the top of a human-skull.
Karaṇḍa- Mukuṭa	:	Coiffure shaped like an inverted jar with tiers of tightly coiled curls.
Kaṭisūtra	:	A thin waist-belt.
Kartrī	:	A kind of chopper
Kāyā- Bandha	:	a sash tied to the waist.
Keyura	:	Armlets of decorative designs.
Khaḍga	:	a kind of sword.
Khandolite	:	a type of stone.
Khapurī	:	Skull, flattish bell shaped member above the *amla*ā
Khaṭvāṅga	:	club formed by the bone of the forearm or leg with a skull at the top.
Kheṭaka	:	Shield, circular or rectangular, with a strap-handle on the back.
khākharā	:	Semi-cylindrical member resembling the local vegetable *Boiti Kakhāru* (pumpkin gourd)
Khukri	:	a type of dagger.
Kirīṭa	:	Crest; crown, *tiara;* diadem.
Kirīṭa- Makuṭa	:	Conical coiffure studded with jewels.
Kīrtimukha	:	'Face of glory'; decorative motif showing the grinning face of a lion with horns; festoons of pearls may drip from its mouth.

Kūcha- Bandha	:	Breast-tie.
Kuṇḍala	:	Ring type ear-ring.
Kuṇḍikā	:	A mendicant's bowl.
Kuthāra	:	Axe.
Lalitāsana	:	Relaxed seated pose with one leg pendent while the other is placed horizontally on the seat beneath the body.
Lambanam	:	a long necklace made of chains held at intervals by flat bands.
Liṅga	:	Male generative organ; the phallic emblem or unmanifest form of Śiva.
Mahiṣhīs	:	She-buffaloes.
Makara Toraṇa	:	Arch with a makara at the base on either side and usually with a Kīrtimukha at the apex.
Maṇi	:	jewell; gem; one of the treasures of a cakravartin (world-ruler).
Mantra	:	Short mystic formula or symbols; however, in defining mantra, Sāstra says "That is called mantra, from manana or meditation of which arises the Universal special knowledge leading to liberation". Mantra- Śuddhi : purification of mantra.
Māyā	:	power of cosmic delusion, in its essence identical to prarkṛti and Śakti, which gives rise to phenomenal appearances.

Mekhalā	:	Waist-band with many more string with clasp and decorative designs at the centre.
Mudgara	:	Hammer.
Mudrā	:	'Seal', hand posture or gesture conveying a specific mystic meaning.
Mudrikā	:	finger-ring.
Mukuṭa	:	Crown.
Mātṛkā	:	The śakti, female counterpart of certain gods, see *saptamatṛkas*
muṇḍamālā	:	Garland of skulls
Mahārājālalitāsana	:	Relaxed seated pose with one leg pendant and the other knee raised where it often supports the arm.
Nāga	:	Serpent, fabulous creature with a human bust, serpent tail and a canopy of serpent hoods. Female counterpart is Nagi.
Nāga- Kuṇḍala	:	snake-like ear-rings.
Nāga- Pāśa	:	a noose formed by a living snake that was viewed in Vedic times as Varuna's own favourite weapon.
Nūpura	:	Anklets with rings or elaborate designs.
Pābhāga	:	'foot'; set of lowermost mouldings at the base of the Temple.
Padmāsana	:	Lotus seat; sitting posture in which legs are crossed and the feet are brought to rest on the thighs; vajraparyānka; yogāsana; dhyānāsana.

paryaṅka	:	A seated pose with one leg resting on the other and the soles turned upwards.
Preta	:	Ghost of a late person, departed soul
Preta-vāhana	:	The corpse acting as mount
Pāga	:	Vertical projections of the bada and gaṇḍi of the temple ratha.
Paraśu	:	Battle axe.
Pārśva- Devatā	:	each of the accessory deities occupying the three outer niches of the central projections of the Vimāna (the main spire-roofed shrine containing the sanctum) of a Hindu temple; they receive worship and arc conncctcd in doctrine with the main divinity of the temple.
Pāśa	:	Noose, fetters.
Paśu- Bali	:	animal sacrifice
Patra- Kuṇḍala	:	circular ear-ring.
Pavī	:	Thunderbolt.
Phaṇi	:	Snake having hood.
Pīṭha	:	base or plinth of temple beneath pābhāga; seat; a centre or place of worship; Śākta temple.
Prabhā	:	Halo.
Prabhāvalī	:	a halo of light; aureole; prabhāmaṇḍala.
Prakṛti	:	Cosmic substance; the uncaused cause of phenomenal existences; nature.
Praṇāma	:	Obeisance.
Pratimā	:	Image.

Pratyāliḍha	:	a particular attitude where the left foot advanced and right drawn back.
Pūjā	:	Worship, ritualistic homage, adoration etc. Pūjāgriha : house where the image is installed.
Puruṣa	:	cosmic man; cosmic spirit; the ultimate principle.
Puṣpa	:	flower.
Rāhā	:	Center vertical projection (pāga) on each side of the deul.
Raudra	:	the terrific.
Rūpa	:	Figures.
Sādhaka	:	Spiritual aspirant.
Sahasrāra- Chakra	:	cerebrum, where a thousand petalled lotus lies on a Plexuses.
Śākta- Maṇḍala	:	Mystic circle or diagram associated with Devī-worship.
Śakti	:	energy; the supreme power, the creative principle; the goddesses and source of existence; spear.
Śaktyāyudha	:	Śakti-weapon.
Samabhaṅga	:	To stand straight without any bend in the body.
Samādhi	:	The final stage in the practice of yoga in which the practitioner, in deep meditation, becomes one with the object of meditation and attains mokṣa.

Śāṅkala	:	Chain.
Śaṅkha	:	Conch.
Sara	:	Arrow.
Sarpa	:	Snake.
Sarpa- Kuṇḍala	:	An earring resembling a coiled serpent.
Sarpa- Maṇḍala	:	a circular snake-coiffure.
Saumya	:	The mild.
Saptamātṛkā	:	The seven divine mother, the most popular images being Brahmānī, Śivānī,Kaumārī, Vaiṣṇavī, Indāṇi, Varāhī, Cāmuṇḍā
Śayana	:	Sleep.
Sitāra	:	a round ornament on forehead.
Śrichakra	:	mystic diagram with several intersected triangles for Devī-worship.
Śūchi - Mudrā	:	a hand posture forming a fist and extending index Finger pointing up and out away from the body.
Sukhāsana	:	an easy seating posture by folding the right foot under the left thigh and left foot under the right thigh.
Śūla	:	Trident; spear.
Śyāma	:	Dark colour.
Taira	:	a designed ornament worn on the forehead.
Tanka	:	Small chisel-like weapon.
Tanu	:	Body.

Tarjanī - Mudrā	: Hand pose with the extended forefinger pointedupward.
Tirthas	: Holy place of pilgrimage.
Tribhaṅga	: Standing pose in which the body has three bends.
Triśūla	: Trident.
Ugra	: A violent form of the Goddess.
Ulūka	: An owl.
Upādāna	: Element.
Upapīṭhas	: Sub-ordinate pīṭhas.
Upavīta	: Sacred thread.
Utpala	: Blossom of Nymphaea caerulea; blue lotus.
Uttarīya	: Cloth for the upper part of the body.
Vāhan	: Mount; vehicle.
Vajra	: Thunderbolt.
Vajra-ghaṇṭā	: a bell shaped weapon having a long handle.
Vajra- Mastaka	: an elaborate double caitya-medalliions crowned by a kirttimukha decorating the Rāhā pāgas of the Vimāna.
Vija-pūraka	: a ball of meal meaning an offering
Valaya	: Wrist-bands.
Vajraparyaṅka	: Seated pose with legs crossed and interlocked the soles of the feet printed upward, *padmāsana*
Vanamāla	: Garland of wild flowers.

Varadā- Mudrā	:	Hand pose of bestowing boons; the arm is lowered and the open palm is turned downwards towards the observer.
Vasana	:	cloth, dress, drapery.
Vigraha	:	Image for worship.
Viśapadma	:	Double petalled lotus seat.
Yogini	:	Ogresses or sorceresses; attendants of Durgā; subsidiary female deities.
Yajñopavīta		
Yoni	:	Female organ of generation.
Yūpa	:	Sacrificial post.

BIBLIOGRAPHY

Primary Sources

Adhyātma Rāmāyaṇa, Gita press, Gorakhpur.

Agni Purāṇa, Ānandāśrama Sanskrit Series, Poona, 1957.

Agni Purāṇa, Tr. by M.N. Dutta, Calcutta, 1903-04.

Amara Kośa, Narela Kishore press, Lahore, 1918.

Aparājita Vāstu Śāstra, Vishvakarmā.

Aparājitapṛcchā, Lal Mani Dubey, Lakṣmī Publications, New Delhi, 1987.

Aparājitapṛcchā: *A Critical Study*, L.M. Dubey, Allahabad, 1987.

Aṣṭadhyayi of Pāṇini, Ed. And Tr. S.C. Vasu, Allahabad, 1891.

Atharva Veda, Ed. S.P.D. Satvalekar, Bombay, 1938.

Bhāgavata Purāṇa, published by Geeta press, Gorakhpur.

Bhaviṣya Purāṇa, Venkatesh Press, Bombay, 1910.

Bhūvana Pradiīpa, Ed. N.K.Bose, Calcutta, 1929.

Brahma Vaivarta Purāṇa, Guru Maṇḍala Granth Mālā and Venkatashwar Press, Bombay, Saṁvat 1988.

Brahmāṇḍa Purāṇa, Venkateshwara press, Bombay, 1923.

Bṛhadāraṇyaka Upaniṣad, with Commentary of S. Acharya, A.S.S. Poone,1915.

Bṛhaddharma Purāṇa, Chaukhamba Amarabhārati Prakāshan, Banaras,1897.

Bṛhat Saṁhitā, Varāha Mihira.

Bṛhata Tantrasāra, Kṛṣṇānanda Āgamavāgisa, Navabharat Publishers, Calcutta.

Caṇḍī Maṅgala, Mukunda Rām, Ed.Sukumar Sen, Calcutta University Publication.

Caṇḍī Purāṇa, Śāral Dāsa, Friends Publisher, Cuttack, 1977.

Chaturvarga Cintāmaṇi, Hemādri, Bibliotheca Indica, Calcutta, 1873-1911.

Devī Pūjā, A Palm-Leaf manuscript (Catalogue No.T/74) in the Orissa State Museum, Bhubaneswar.

Devī Purāṇa, Ed. Pañcānana, Bangvāsi Press, Calcutta, 1909.

Devī-Bhāgavata Purāṇa, Paṇḍ ita Pustakālaya, Banaras, 1969.

Devī-Bhāgavata, Guru Maṇḍ al Series, Calcutta, 1960.

Devī-Mahātmya, V. S. Agrawal, Allahabad, 1963.

Durgāpūjā Paddhati, a palm-leaf manuscript possessed by Mrityunjaya Rath, village Rāmeśvara, dist- Khurda.

Durgā Sapta Śatī, Swāmi Jagdishwarānanda, Sri Ramakrishna Math, Madras, 1955.

Durgā Tantra Śāstra, Laxmi Nārāyaṇa Goswāmi, Dīp Publication. Agra, 1997.

Durgāpūjā Paddhati, a palm-leaf manuscript possessed by Liṅgarāja Mishra, village-Chandramā Pāttapur, dist-Puri.

Durgāyajanadīpika, Jagannatha Acharya, a palm-leaf manuscript (Catalogue No.T/5) in the Orissa State Museum, Bhubaneswar.

Durgotsavacandrikā, a plam-leaf manuscript possessed by Chandrasekhar Samantary, temple Priest of Lord Kapileśvara, village-Dia, dist-Khurda.

Durgotsavacandrikā, Rama Chandra Gajapati, A Palm-Leaf manuscript (CatalogueNo.T/82) in the Orissa State Museum, Bhubaneswar.

Durgotsavacandrikā, Vardhana Mahapatra, A Palm-Leaf manuscript (Catalogue No.T/51 & T/81) in the Orissa State Museum, Bhubaneswar.

Durgotsavapūjā, A Palm-Leaf manuscript (Catalogue No.T/100) in the Orissa State Museum, Bhubaneswar.

Ekāmra Candrikā, Ed. R.Gargavatu, Cuttack, 1931.

Ekāmra Purāṇa, Ed. L.Gargavatu, Cuttack, 1933.

Garuḍa Purāṇa, Ed. M.N.Dutt, Calcutta, 1908;Ed. Pansikar, Bombay, 1924; Ed. R.S. Bhattacharya, Benaras,1894.

Gautama Dharma Sūtra, L. Srinivasacarya, Mysore, 1917.

Halāyudhakośa, Ed. Chaukhambha Sanskrit Series.

Harivaṁśa Purāṇa, Ed. Ramachandra Shastri, Oriental Research Institute, Poona,1936.

Harivaṁśa Purāṇa, Gita press, Gorakhpur.

Hevajra Tantra: A Critical Study,Introduction and Tr. D.L. Snellgrove, London, 1959.

Iśaṇa Śiva Gurudeva Paddhati, T.S.S., Trivandrum, 1920-24.

Jñānārṇava Tantra, Ānanda Āśrama Series, 1912.

Kālīkā Purāṇa, Venkateshwar Press, Bombay, Saṁvat, 1964.

Kāmikāgama, MS No. D5431, Government Oriental manuscript Library, Madras.

Kathāsaritsāgara of Somadeva, Tr. By C.H. Tawney, (Ed.) N.M. Penzer, London,1924.

Kaulārṇava Tantra, T.T.S, Calcutta, 1917.

Kena Upaniṣad, Bombay, 1927.

Kulacūḍāmaṇi Nigama, Ed.Arthur Avalon, Madras, 1956.

Kulārṇava Tantra, Ed. John Woodroffe, A. Avalon and M.P.Pundit, Madras, 1965.

Kurma Purāṇa, Guru Maṇḍ al Series, Calcutta, 1962.

Liṅga Purāṇa, Ed. J.V. Bhattacharya, Calcutta, 1885.

Liṅga Purāṇa, Guru Maṇḍ al Series, Calcutta, 1960.

Mādalāpānji, Ed. Mohanty, A.B., Utkal University, 1960.

Mahābhārata, Ed. By Satvaleka, Ajmavedic Press, 1940.

Mahābhārata, Tr. M.N. Dutt, (Banga Vasi Edition) Calcutta, 1895-1905; Tr. P.C.Ray (new edition), Calcutta, 1926-32.

Mahānirvāṇa Tantra, Gita Press, Gorakhpur

MahānirvāṇaTantra, John Woodroffe, Madras,1985.

Mānasāra, Ed. P.K. Acharya, London, 1932.

Manasollāsa ____________of Bhaṭṭa Someśvara, Mysore,1926.

Manusmṛti, Choukhamba Sanskrit Series, Benaras, 1935.

Mārkaṇḍeya Purāṇa, V.S. Agrawal, *A study*, Allahabad, 1961.

Mārkaṇḍeya Purāṇa, Ed. K.M. Banerjee, Calcutta, 1862 Tr. F.E. Pargiter, Calcutta,1904.

Mātṛkā Bheda Tantra, Ed. By C. Bhattacharya, Calcutta, 1933.

Matsya Purāṇa, Ed. H.N. Apte, A.S.S, Poone, 1907.

Matsya Purāṇa, Translated by H.H.Wilson.

Meru Tantra, N.S.P., Bombay, 1908.

Muṇḍaka Upaniṣad, Ed. Nirnaya Sagara Press, Bombay, 1918.

Nātya Śāstra of Bharat Muni, Tr. M.M. Ghosh, Calcutta, 1967.

Nityaṣoḍaśikārṇava, Ed. V.V. Dviveda (S.S.V); Yogatantra Grantha Mālā, Benaras,1905.

Odishāra Debādevī, Odisha Book Store, Binodbihari, Cuttack, 1980.

Odishāra Śākta Saṁskruti, Odisha Cultural Forum, 1980.

Padma Purāṇa, Bengal Printing Works, Calcutta, 1959.

Prāchi Mahātmya, Dvija Trilochana, Cuttack, 1898.

Prāṇa Toṣinī, Rām Toshana Bhattacharya, Calcutta, 1898.

Prapañcasāra Tantra, Ed. By A.Avalon, 1935.

Prapañcasārasāra Saṁngraha, Govind Chandra Sarasvatī.

Prapañcasāratantraṁ. Ed. Atalānanda Sarasvatī, Motial Banarsidass, Delhi, 1981.

Raghuvaṁśa, Ed. H.D. Valenkar, Bombay, 1948.

Rāmāyaṇa, Ed. J.M. Mehta and Others, Oriental Institute, Baroda, 1960.

Rāmāyaṇa, Ed. N.Rāmaratnam, Madras, 1958.

Ṛgveda Saṁhitā, Ajmer Vedic Press, Saṁvat, 1973. Ed. Satvalekar, 1940.

Ṛgveda, Ed. N.S. Sontakke and C.G. Kashikar Poona: Vaidika Saṁsodhana Maṇḍ ala,1933-51.

Rudra Yāmala Tantra, Ed. By Ramchandra Kak, Kashmir, 1941.

Rūpamaṇḍana, Ed. Balaram Srivastav, Motilal Banarsidass, Delhi, 1992.

Śabda Kalpa Drumaḥ, Choukhamba Sanskrit Series Varanasi, 1961.

Sādhanamālā, Ed., Benoytosh Bhattacharyya, 2 Vols., Baroda, 1968.

Śākta Pramoda, Ed. Sri Venkateśvara Press, Bombay, 1951.

Śākta Upaniṣads, Ed. A.M. Sastri, the Adyar Library, 1950.

Śakti Aṅka Kalyāna, Gita Press, Gorakhpur, 1934.

Śakti Saṅgam Tantra, Ed. B. Bhattacharya, Oriental Institute, Baroda, 1932, 1941,1947.

Śāradā Tilaka Tantram, Tr., A Board of Scholars, Delhi, 1988.

Śāradā Tilakam, Chamanlal Gautam, Bareli, 1985.

Śāradāsaradarcchana Paddhati, Godavara Mahapatra, a palm-leaf manuscript (Catalogue No.T/13) in the Orissa State Museum, Bhubaneswar.

Śatapatha Brāhmaṇa, Achuta Grantha Mālā, Kashi, S.1994.

Śatapatha Brāhmaṇa, Ed. Albrecht Weber, Chouakhamba Sanskrit Series, Banaras,1964.

Saundaryalaharī, Ed. S.S. Sastri, Adyar, 1937, Oriental Institute, Baroda, 1941.

Śilpa Prakāsa, Rama Chandra Kaulācāra Tr. Alice Boner and Sadasiva Ratha Sarmā, Leiden, 1966.

Śilparatna, T.S.S, Trivandrum, 1922.

Śiva Mahā Purāṇa, Nag Publishers, Delhi.

Śiva Purāṇa, Tr. A Board of Scholars, Motilal Banarsidass, Delhi, 1970.

Skanda Purāṇa, Guru Maṇḍ al Series, Calcutta, 1962.

Skanda Purāṇa, Mansukharaja Mora, Calcutta,1959-62.

Ślipa Śāstra, Kasyapa, Saraswati Mahal Publications, Tanjore.

Śvetāśvataropaniṣad, Swāmi Tyagiśānanda, Sri Ramakrishna math, Mylapore, 1959.

Śyāmārcchanataraṅgiṇī, A palm-leaf manuscript possessed by Narasimha Mahapatra, village-Maitratrilocanpur, dist-Puri.

Taittirīya Āraṇyaka, Ānanda Āśrama Series, Poona,1967-69.

Taittirīya Brāhmaṇa, Ānanda Āśrama Series, Poona, 1934-38.

Tantra Yoga, Nik Douglas, Munshiram Manoharlal, New Delhi, 1971.

Tatttirīya Saṁhitā, Ānanda Āśrama Series, Poona.

The Śākta Upanisads, Tr. A.G. Krisna Warrier, Adyar Library and Research Center, Madras:1964.

The Saundaryalahari or Flood of Beauty, Ed and Tr. W.Norman Brown, Mass: Harvard University Press, Cambridge,1958.

Tripurā Rahasya, Mahātmya Khaṇḍa, Choukhamba Sanskrit Series, Benaras, Saṁvat,1988.

Vājasaneyiī Saṁhitā, Nirnaya Sagara Press, 1928.

Vājasaneyiī Saṁhitā, V.L. Shastri Panikhar, Bombay, 1912.

Vāmana Purāṇa, Ed. Anand Swarup Gupta, Tr. S. M. Mukhopadhyaya and Others All India Kashiraj Trust, Banaras,1968.

Varāha Purāṇa, Gita press, Gorakhpur.

Varāha Purāṇa, Ed. H. Sastri Calcutta, 1893.

Vāstu Śāstra, D.N. Shuklā, Gorakhpur University, 1958.

Vāyu Purāṇa, Ed. R.L. Mitra Calcutta 1880-86,Ed. M.C. Apte A.S.S., Poone,1905-1907.

Vāyu Purāṇa, Venkateśvara Press, Bombay, Saṁvat, 1933.

Viṣṇu Dharmottara Purāṇa, Sri Venkateśvara Press, Bombay, 1938.

Viṣṇu Purāṇa, Tr. H.H. Wilson, Punthi Pustak, Calcutta, 1961.

Viśvakarmāvatāra Śāstra, Trivandrum Sanskrit Series.

Yoginīhṛdaya, Ed. Gopinath Kaviraja, Banaras, 1924.

Secondary Sourse

Acharya, K., *Ekāmra Kṣhetra, Bhubaneswar*, Utkal Pāṭhak Saṁsad(Ed), Kedār Gourī, Cuttack, 1993.

Acharya, P, "Alāpur Plates of Narasiṁha II, Śaka Year 1215", *Epigraphia Indica*, Vol. XXXI, No.3, 1955.

-------------, "The Commemorative Inscription of the Ananta-Vāsudeva Temple at Bhubaneswar", *O.H.R.J.*, Vol.I, No.4, 1953.

-------------, "Varieties of Stones used in Building Temples and Making Images in Orissa", *O.H.R.J.*, Vol.XIII, 1905.

-------------, "Studies in Temple Architecture in Orissa", *O.H.R.J.*, Vol XII,1964.

-------------, "Triliṅga, Trikaliṅga, Kaliṅga, Oḍra and Utkal", *O.H.R.J.*, Vol I, 1953.

-------------, *Studies in Orissa History, Archaeology*, Baripada, 1969.

-------------, *Studies in the History, Archaeology and Archives*, Cuttack, 1969.

Acharya, P.K., *Architecture of Mānasāra*, Oxford, 1933.

-------------, *Dictionary of Hindu Architecture*, Delhi, 1979.

-------------, *Goddesses in Ancient India; Abhinava Publications*, New Delhi, 1984.

-------------, Hindu *Architecture in India and Abroad,* Mānasāra Series Vol.VI, Allahabad, 1946.

-------------, *Indian Architecture According to Mānasāra Ślpaśātra*, Mānasāra Series Vol. II, Allahabad, 1927.

Agrawal, P.K., *The Goddesses of Ancient India*, Delhi,1984.

-------------,*Gupta Temple Architecture*, Benaras,1969.

Agrawal, Urmila, *Khajuraho Sculptures & Their Significance*, New Delhi, 1964.

Agrawal,V. S., *Devī-Mahātmya*, Allahabad, 1963.

-------------, *Indian Art, Benaras, 1960.*

-------------, *Mārkaṇḍeya Purāṇa-A study*, Allahabad, 1961.

Agrawala, R.C., "Ambicā temple at Jagat", *Arts Asiatiques*, Vol.X.1964.

-------------, 'Nārāyaṇī and Dancing Durgā in Indian Sculpture', *O.H.R.J,* Vol. XIV,no.1(1969).

-------------, "A Terracotta plaque of Mahiṣāsuramardinī from Nagar, Rajasthan", *Lalit Kala*, Nos.1&2.

-------------, "Goddess Mahiṣāsuramardinī in Early India Art*", Artibus Asia*, Vol.XXI, 1958.

Agrawala, V.S., *Divīmahātmya*: The Glorification of the Great Goddess, Varanasi,1963.

-------------, *Vāmaṇa Purāṇa*: *A Study,* Prithivi Prakashan,Varanasi,1964.

Anderson, J., *Catalogue and Hand Book of the Archaeological Collections in the Indian Musum*, Calcutta, 1983.

Apte, V.M., *Social and Religious Life in the Grhya Sutra*, Bombay, 1954.

Apte, V.S., *The Students Sanskrit-English Dictonary*, Motilal Banarsidass, Delhi, 1963.

Aryan, K.C., *The Little Goddesses* (*Mātṛkās*), New Delhi, 1980.

Avalon, Arthur(Ed), *Principles of Tantra*, Madras, 1960.

-------------(Ed), *Kūlacudāmaṇi Nigama*, Madras, 1956.

-------------, and Ellen Avalon, *Hymns to the Goddess,* Madras, 1964.

-------------, *Introduction to Tantra Sastra*, Madras, 1969.

-------------, *The Garland of Letters 7th* (Ed), Madras.

Awasthi, A.B.S., Studies in Skanda Purāṇa, Lucknow, 1966.

Bagchi P.C., *Studies in the Tantras*, Vol.I, Calcutta, 1939.

Bagchi Subhendugopal, *Eminent Indian Śākta Centers in Eastern India*, Calcutta, 1980.

Bajpei, K.D., "Mahakosala in Ancient Literature", *P.I.H.C*, Vol.IX.

-------------, *Archaeology in Uttar Pradesh*, Lucknow,1957.

Bala, Subramaniam, *Early Chola Art*, Bombay, 1968.

Banarjee, A.K., *Discourses on Hindu Spiritural Culture, II*, Ramashram Satsang, Sikandarabad, Uttar Pradesh, 1971.

Bandyopadhyaya, Pranab, *Mother Goddess Durgā, Calcutta*, 1987, p. 66.

Banerjee, J.N., *The Development of Hindu Iconography*, University Press, Calcutta, 1941.

..............., *The Development of Hindu Iconography*, Calcutta, 1956.

-------------, "Some Folk Goddesses of Ancient and Medieval India", *I.H.Q.*, Vol.14, 1938.

-------------, *Puranic and Tantric Religion*, Calcutta, 1966.

-------------, *Religious Art and Archaeology*, Lucknow, 1968.

-------------, *The Development of Hindu Iconography*, New Delhi, 1985.

Banerjee, R.D., "Antiquities of Baudh State", *J.B.O.R.S.*, Vol. XV, 1929.

-------------, *Eastern Indian School of Medieval Sculpture, A.S.I.*, Vol.47, Delhi, 1933.

-------------, *History of Orissa*, 2 Vols, Calcutta, 1931.

Banerji, M., "Aryan Attitude to Female Deities", *J.B.O.R.S*, Vol.XXV, pt.1, March, 1939.

Barneth Kempers, *Ancient Indian Arts*, Masachusetts, 1959.

Barrett, A., *Early Chola Architecture*, 806-1014 A.D. London, 1974.

-------------, "A Terracotta Plaque of Mahiṣāsuramardinī", *Oriental Art*, XXI, 1975-76.

Barua, B.K., *A Cultural History of Assam*, Calcutta, 1951.

Basham, A.l., *The Wonder That Was India*, New York, 1968.

Beane,W., *Myth Cult and Symbols in Śākta Hinduism:A Study of the Indian Mother Goddess,* Leiden,1977.

Beglar, J.D., "Report of Tours in South- Eastern Provinces, pp. 1874-75 and 1875-76". *A.S.I*, XII, 1876.

Behera, K.S., *Temples of Orissa*, Bhubaneswar,1993.

-------------, "Brahmanical Temples of Orissa" *Orissa review: Monumental Special*, Ed. A.N. Tiwari, Cuttack, 1976.

-------------, "The Evolution of Śakti Cult at Jājpur, Bhubanswar and Puri", *the Śakti Cult and Tārā*, Ed. D.C. Sircar, University of Calcutta, Calcutta, 1967.

-------------, "Three images of Mahiṣāsuramardinī from Orissa", Proc. *Ind. Congress*, XXVII, 1967.

-------------, & Donaldson, *Sculpture Masterpieces from Orissa: Style and Iconography*, New Delhi, 1998.

Behera, S.C., *Rise and fall of Sailodbhavas*, Calcutta, 1982.

Bhandarkar, R.G., *Early History of Decan*, Calcutta, 1957.

-------------, Vaishnavism, *Saivism and Minor Religious Systems*, Varanasi, 1945.

Bhardwaj, Surinder Mohan. *Hindu Place of Pilgrimage in India,* Berkeley, Los Angeles,

University of California Press, London, 1973.

Bhattacharjee, A., *Icons and Sculptures of Early and Medieval Assam,* Delhi, 1978.

Bhattacharya, Benoytosh, Ed., *Śaktisaṅgama Tantra*. Oriental Institute, Baroda, 1941.

Bhattacharya, N.N., *Indian Mother Goddess*, New Delhi, 1977.

-------------, *History of the Śākta Religion*, Munshiram Manoharlal Publishers, New Delhi, 1974.

Bhattacharyya, Dipak Chandra, *Iconography of Composite Images,* New Delhi, 1980.

-------------, *Pratimālakṣaṇ of the Viṣṇudharmottara*, New Delhi, 1991.

Bhattasali, Nalini Kanta, *Iconography of Buddhist and Brahmanical Sculptures in the Dacca Museum,* Indological Book House, Varanasi, 1972.

Boal, B.M., *the konds: Human Sacrifice and Religious Change*, Bhubaneswar, 1984.

Boner, A., *Principles of Composition in Hindu Sculptures*, Leiden, 1962.

-------------, Sadasiva Rath Sarma and R.P. Das, *New Light on the Sun temple of Konarka*, Varanasi, 1972.

Bose, N.K., *Canons of Orissan Architecture*, Calcutta, 1932.

-------------, *Culture and Society in Orissa*, Calcutta, 1967.

-------------, *Principles of India Śilpa Śāstra*, Delhi, 1978.

Brighenti, Francesco, *Śakti Cult in Orissa*, New Delhi, 2001.

Brown, Percy, *Indian Architecture: Buddist and Hindu Periods*, Bombay, 1965.

Burgess, J., *Ancient Monument, Temples and Sculptures Of India*, 2.Vols, London, 1897-1911.

-------------, *Architectural Antiquities of Western India*, London, 1903.

Campbell Joseph., *The Art of Indian Asia*, I-II, New York, 1955.

Chakravarti, P.C., *Doctrine of Śakti in Indian Literature*, New Delhi, 1940.

Chakravarti,C.H., *Tantras: Studies on Their Religion and Literture*, Punthi Pustak, Calcutta, 1963.

Chanda, R.P., "Exploration in Orissa," *MASI*, No.44,1930.

-------------, *Medieval Indian Sculptures in British Museum*, London, 1937.

Chattopadhyaya, S., *Early History of North India*, Calcutta, 1970.

Chawdhri, L.R., *Secrets of Yantra Mantra and Tantra*, Sterling Publishers, New Delhi,1992.

Coburn, Thomas B., *Devī-Mahātmya: The Crystallization of the Goddess Tradition, Delhi, 1984*.

Coomaraswamy, A.K., *Art of India & Ceylon*, New York, 1905.

-------------, *Early Indian Iconography, Eastern Art*, Philadelphia, 1928.

-------------, *History of Indian and Indonesian Art*, London, 1927.

-------------, *Introduction to Indian Art*, New Delhi, 1969.

Crooke, W., *Popular Religions and Folklore in Northern India*, Westminster, 1896.

Cunningham, Alexander, *The Ancient Geography of India*, Benaras, 1963.

-------------, *Archaeological Survey of India Report*, Vol. IX and Vol.XIII.

Das, Biswarup, *The Bhaumākara Buddhist Kings of Orissa and Their Times*, New Delhi, 1978.

-------------,*Orissa:Social Cultural and Religious Aspects*, Delhi, 1985.

Das, D., *The Early History of Kalinga, a Socio-Economic and Cultural History of Coastal Orissa*, Calcutta, 1977.

Das, D.R., *Temples of Orissa: A study of Sub-Style*, New Delhi, 1982.

Das, H. C., *Śākta Pīṭhas: A Study*, Bhubaneswar, 1999.

-------------, *Cultural Development of Orissa*, Calcutta, 1985.

-------------, *Iconography Of Śākta Divinities*, 2 Vols, New Delhi, 1997.

-------------, *Tantricism: A Study of the Yogini Cult*, New Delhi, 1981.

Das, M., *Temples of India*, Bombay, 1970.

Das, M.N. Ed., *Sidelights on History and Culture of Orissa*, Cuttack, 1977.

Das, R.K., *Temples of Tamilnadu*, Bombay, pp.49-50, 1964.

Das, Sudhendukumar, *Śakti or Divine Power,* University of Calcutta, Calcutta, 1934.

Dasgupta.S.P., *Obscure Religious Cult*, Calcutta,1976.

Dash, M.P., "Worship of Saptamatṛkās and their Representation in Orissan Temples", *O.H.R.J.,* Vol. XI, No.2, 1962.

-------------(Ed), *A Descriptive Catalogue of Sanskrit Manuscripts in the Orissa State Museum*, Vol.V, Bhubaneswar, 1965.

Dehejia, Vidya, *Early Stone Temple of Orissa*, New Delhi, 1979.

-------------, *Yogini Cult and Temples: A Tantric Tradition*, New Delhi, 1986.

Desai, Devangana, *Erotic Sculpture from India*,new Delhi,1975.

Deva, K., *Temples of North India*, New Delhi, 1969.

Dhal, U.N., *Goddess Lakṣmi, Origin and Development*, Oriental Publishers, New Delhi, 1978.

-------------, *Mahiṣāsura in Art and Thought*, Delhi, 1991.

Dikshit, S.K., *Mother Goddess*, Poona, 1943.

Donaldson, T. E., *Hindu Temple Art of Orissa*,3 Vols, Leiden, 1985-87.

-------------, *Tantra and Śākta Art Of Orissa*,3 Vols, New Delhi, 2002.

-------------, "Beautiful & Terrifying Śākta Images of Orissa," *Arts of Asia*, Vol.13, No.1, Hong Kong, 1983.

-------------, "Some Little- Known Metal Images from Orissa," *Art of Asia*, Vol.18, No.1, 1988.

-------------, and R.P. Mohapatra, *Ornaments of Orissa*, Delhi, 1998.

Dubey, Arthur Avalon, (Rd), *Kūlacudāmaṇi Nigama* Madras, 1956.

Eishmann, A. Kulke, H. And Tripathy, G.C. (Eds.), *The Cult of Jagannath and Regional traditions of Orissa*, New Delhi, 1978.

Eliot, H.M., *History of India as told by its own Historians*, Calcutta, 1955.

Elwin Verrier, *The Tribal Art of Middle India*, London, 1951.

-------------, Tribal Myths of Orissa, Oxford, London, 1954.

Fabri, Charls, *A History of Indian Dress*, Calcutta, 1960.

-------------, *History of the Art of Orissa*, New Delhi, 1974.

Farkhuhar, J. N., *An Outline of the Religious Literature of India*, Oxford, 1920.

Fergusson James, *Tree and Serpent Worship in Ancient India*, London, 1873.

Ferusson, J.H., A History of Indian and eastern Architecture, 2 Vols, London, 1920.

Fousbell, V., *Indian Mythology*, London, 1902.

Fredric, L., *Indian Temples and Sculptures*, London, 1959.

Gangoly, Orhendra and A. Goswami, *Orissan Sculpture and Architecture*,

Calcutta,1956.

Ganguly, Manmohan, *Orissa and Her Remains*, Calcutta, 1912.

Gargabatu, R., *Ekāmra Purāṇa*, Cuttack, 1931.

Ghosha, Pratapachandra, *Durgā Pūjā: with Notes and Illustrations,* Hindoo Patriot Press, Calcutta, 1871.

Ghosha, U.N., *Studies in Indian History and Culture*, Orient Longman, Bombay,1965.

Goswamy, A., *Indian Temple Sculpture*, Calcutta, 1926.

Gupta, R.S., *Iconography of the Hindus, Buddhists and Jains*, Taraporevela Sons& Co,Bombay, 1972.

Harle, J.C., "On a Dispute Element in the Iconography of Early Mahiṣāsuramardinī Images," *Arts Orientals*, 1970.

-------------, "On the Mahiṣāsuramardinī Images of the Udaigiri Hills(Vidisha) Caves", *Journal of Indian Society of Oriental Art*, IV, 1971-72.

-------------, *Gupta Sculpture*, Oxford, 1974.

Havel, E.V., *Handbook of Indian Art*, London, 1911.

-------------, *The Ideals of Indian Art*, London, 1920.

Hazra, R.C., *Studies in the UpaPurāṇas,* Vol. II, Calcutta Sanskrit College Research Series, Calcutta, 1963.

-------------, *Studies in the Purnic Records on Hindu Rites and Customs,* Delhi, 1987.

Hota, Nihar Ranjan, "Human Sacrifices among the Khonds of Orissa", *O.H.R.J,* Vol. VIII, No.3-4,1960.

Hultzsch, E., "Inscriptions of Ashok", *Corpus Inscriptionum Indicarum*, Vol. I, London, 1925.

Hunter, W.W., Andrew Stirtling, John Beams and N.K. Sahu, *A History of Orissa*, 2 Vols. Delhi, 1980.

Iyer K. Bhartha, "An Early Seal of Mahiṣāsuramardinī", *A.A*, XXXI, 1969.

James, E.O., *Prehistoric Religion*, New York, 1959.

-------------, *The Cult of the Mother Goddess*, London, 1959,

Jhavery, Mohanlal Bhagwandas, *Comparative and Critical Study of Mantraśāstra*, Ahmedabad, 1944.

Joanna, G., Williams (Ed), *Kalādarśana*, (American Studies in the Art of India), New Delhi, 1981.

-------------, Williams., *The Art of Gupta India*, New Delhi, 1983.

Joshi, A., *History and Culture of Khijjingakotta*, Delhi, 1983.

-------------, *New Light on the Culture of Orissa*, Cuttack, 1979.

Kane, Pandurang Vaman. *History of Dharmasastra,* 5 vols, Bhandarkar Oriental Insititute, Poona, 1930-62.

Karl Khannalawala, *Indian Sculpture and Paintings*, Bombya, 1987.

Keith, A.B., *Religion and Philosophy of the Vedas and Upanishads*, Oxford, 1925.

Kinsley, David, *Hindu Goddesses*, Delhi, 1986.

Kramarsch, Stella, *Indian Sculptures*, First Indian Reprint, New Delhi, 1981.

-------------, *The Art of India*, New York, 1954.

-------------, *The Hindu Temples*, 2 Vols., Calcutta, 1946.

Kṛṣnananda Āgamavāgisa, *Bṛhat Tantrasāra*, 2 Vols, Basumati Sahitya Mandir, Calcutta,1972.

Kulke, Hermann and G.C. Tripathi(Eds)., *Religion and Society in Eastern India*, New Delhi, 1994.

-------------, "Jagannath as the State Deity of Orissa", *Utkal University Bulletin of History Seminar,* No.1, 1983-4.

Kumar, Pushpendra, *Śakti and Her Episodes*, Delhi, 1986.

-------------, *Śakti Cult in Ancient India*, Bhartiya Publishing House, Varanasi, 1974.

Lal, Kanwar, *Temples and Sculptures of Bhubaneswar*, New Delhi, 1970.

Lalye, P.G., *Studies in Devī Bhāgavata*, Bombay, 1973.

Lannoy, Richard, *The Speaking Tree: A Study of Indian culture and Society,* Oxford University Press, London, 1971.

Law, B.C., *Historical Geography of Ancient India*, Paris, 1954.

Macdonell, A.A., *Vedic Mythology*, Strassburg, 1897.

MacKay, E.J.H. *Further Excavation at Mohenjodaro*, 2vols, Government of India press, Delhi, 1938.

Mackay,E., *Early Indus Civilization*, London, 1935.

Mackenzie, *Indian Myth of Legend*, London, 1980.

Mahapatra, K.N., "A Note on the Hypaethral Temple of Sixty-Four Yoginis at Hirapur", *O.H.R.J.*, Vol. II, 1953.

-------------, "Antiquity of Jagannath Puri as a Place of Pilgrimage" *O.H.R.J.* Vol. III, No.1, 1954.

-------------, "Excavation at Belkhandi in Kalahandi State", *OH.R.J.* (Commemoration Volume),1982.

-------------,*Puranic Stories in the Early Records and Sculptures of Orissa*, *O.H.R.J.*, Vol.X, 1962.

Mahapatra, Manamohan, *Traditional Structure and Change in an Orissan Temple* Calcutta, 1981.

Mahapatra, Sanjaya Kumar, *Khakharā Temples*, Sharada Publishing House, Delhi, 2016.

--------------, *Mahiṣāsuramardinī in Art,Iconography* and Cult Practices, Agam Kala Prakashan, Delhi, 2014.

---------------, *Cāmuṇḍā in Mythology, Art and Iconography*, Agam Kala Pakashan, Delhi,2015.

Mahtab, H. K., *The History of Orissa*, 2 Vols., Cuttack, 1959.

-------------(Ed)., *Glimpses of Orissan Art and Culture*, Bhubaneswar, 1984.

Majumdar, R.C., "Physical Features of Orissa", *J.A.I.H.*, Vol I.

-------------, "Sailodbhava Dynasty", *J.A.H.R.S*, Vol X.

-------------, "Sources of Early History of Orissa", *J.A.I.H.*, Vol I.

-------------, "The Epochs of Ganga Era", *I.H.Q.*, Vol. LXXVI.

Marshall, John Ed., *Mohenjodaro and Indus Civilization*, Vol. I, London, 1931.

Mishra, Binayak, "Trikalinga Dynasty", *J.B.O.R.S.*, Vol XIV.

-------------,*Orissa under Bhaumakra Kings*, Calcutta, 1934.

Mishra, K.C., *The Cult of Jagannatha*, Calcutta, 1971 & 1984.

Mishra, P.K., *Evolution of Orissa and Her Culture*, Sambalpur, 1984.

------------- and Samal, J.K., Eds, *Comprehensive History of Orissa*, 2 Vols, New Delhi, 1997.

Mishra, R.N, *Bharatiya Moorti Kalā* (Hindi),New Delhi,1977.

Mishra, V., *Mahishasuramardini*, Rajesh Publications, Delhi, 1984.

Misra, O.P, *Iconography of the Saptamatrikas*, Agam Kala Prakashan, Delhi, 1989

Mitra R.L., *The Antiquities of Orissa*, Vol.II, Calcutta, 1963.

Mitra, Debala, "Four Little-Known Khākharā Temples of Orissa," *J.A.S.B*, Vol. II, 1960.

-------------, *Bhubaneswar*, New Delhi, 1961.

-------------, *Bronzes from Achutrajpur,Orissa*, Delhi, 1978.

Mitra, R.L., *Antiquities of Orissa*, 2 Vols., Calcutta, 1875 (Reprint, 1961).

Mohapatra, R.P., *Archaeology in Orissa*, 2 Vols., Delhi, 1986.

-------------, *Temple Legends of Orissa*, Bhubaneswar, 1989.

------------- and Thomas Donaldson, *Ornaments of Orissa*, Delhi, 1998.

Mookerjee, Ajit. *Tantra Art: Its Philosophy and Physics*, New Delhi, 1966.

Morgan, K.W., *The Religion of the Hindus*, New York, 1953.

Morley, Grace, *Indian Sculpture*, Varanasi, 1985.

Mukherjee, P.K., "Human Sacrifices among the Khonds of Orissa- A Note", *O.H.R.J.*,Vol. VIII, Nos. 3&4,1960.

-------------, *Hindu Civilization*, Bombay, 1959.

-------------, *The History of Gajapati Kings of Orissa*, Calcutta, 1953.

Nagar, S.L., *Mahishasuramardini in Indian Art*, New Delhi, 1988.

-------------, *The Universal Mother*, Delhi, 1989.

Nagaswami, R., *Tantric Cults of India*, Delhi, 1982.

-------------, *Tantric Cult of South India*, Agamakala Prakashan, Delhi, 1982.

Nath, B.V., 'The Pārvatī Temple Inscription Bhubaneswar', *O.H.R.J.*, Vol.III, No.3, 1954.

Neumann, Erich, *The Great Mother*, New York, 1963.

Oflaherty, Wendy Doniger, *Hindu Myths*, Harmondsworth, 1984.

Oldham, C.F., *The Sun and the Serpent*, London, 1905.

Padhi, Ekadashi, *The Cultural Heritage of Jajpur*, Puri. 2004.

Pal, P., *Hindu Religion and Iconology According to the Tantrasāra*,LosAngeles, 1981

----------- *The Mother Goddesses* According to the *Devipurana* in Singh, Nagendra Kumar, *Encyclopaedia of Hinduism*, Anmol Publications, New Delhi,1941

Panda, L.k., *Saivism in Orissa*, Delhi, 1985.

Panda, S. S., "Archaeological Remains of Bolangir District", *O.H.R.J.*, Vol. XXXVI,No.3-4, 1991.

-------------, "Durgā Icons of the Upper Mahanadi Valley of Orissa", *Orissa Review*, Vol. XLV, No3,1988.

-------------, "Some Temple Ruins of Kalahandi District", *O.H.R.J.*, Vol. XXXVIII, No.1-4, 1993.

Pandit, M.P., *Gems from the Tantras*,Madras,1975.

-------------, *Lights on the Tantra*, Madras, 1977.

Panigrahi, K. C., *Archaeological Remains at Bhubaneswar*, Oriental Longmans, 1961.

-------------, *History of Orissa* (Hindu Period), Cuttack, 1981.

-------------, *Jajpur in the Culture and History of Orissa* (Oriya), Jajpur in the lecturer, Jajpur, 1973.

-------------, "Bhauma Art and Architecture of Orissa", *A.A.*, Vol, IV, 1957.

Panigrahi, Kunjabehari. "Bhadrak Incraption of Gana", *I.H.Q.*, Vol. XXXV, No.3, 1959.

Pargiter, F.E., *Ancient Indian Historical Tradition*, London, 1912, Indian Reprint, New Delhi, 1972.

-------------, Tr.,*Mārkaṇḍeya Purāṇa*, Delhi,1969.

Patel, C.B., *Dynastic History of Nalas*, Calcutta, 1990.

Pathak, V., *History of Kosala*, Banaras, 1963.

Patil, D. R., *Monuments of The Udayagiri Hill,* Gwalior, 1958.

Patnaik, D. N., *Festivals of Orissa*, Bhubaneswar, 1982.

Patnaik, J.K., "Temples of South Kosala (6th century A.D.-11th century A.D.)": *A Case Study of Stellate Temples*, Ph.D. Thesis, Sambalpur Unversity, 1998.

Payne, Ernest Alexander*, The Śāktas, Calcutta*, YMCA publishing House, 1933.

Piggott, Stuart, *Prehistoric India,* Penguin Books, Harmonds Worth, 1950.

Pradhan, B. C., "Śakti worship in Orissa", Ph. D. Dissertation, Sambalpur University, 1983.

Pradhan, S., "Siddheśvara Temple at Palāri", *Souvenir of O.H.C.* (Silver Jubilee Session), Sambalpur Unversity, 1996.

-------------(Ed), *Art and Archaeology of Orissa Recent Perspectives*, New Delhi, 2006.

-------------, *Rock Art in Orissa*, New Delhi, 2001.

Preston, James J., *The Cult of the Goddess: Social and Religious Change in a Hindu Temple*, Vikas Publishing House, New Delhi, 1980.

Rajaguru, Satyanarayana, *History of the Gaṅgas*, 2 Vols., Bhubaneswar, 1968-72.

-------------, *Inscriptions of Orissa*, Vol. I, part II, Berhampur, 1958.

-------------, *Inscriptions of Orissa*, Vol. III, part II, Bhubaneswar, 1960.

-------------, *Inscriptions of Orissa*, Vol. IV, Bhubaneswar, 1966.

-------------, "A Historical Account of Virajā-Keṣtra from Inscriptions", *O.H.R.J*, Vols. XXIV, XXV,XXVI,1980.

Rajan, K.V.S., *Early Kalingan Art and Architecture*, New Delhi, 1984.

Rajeswari, D. R., *Śakti Iconography*, New Delhi, 1989.

Rao, Gopinath, T.A., *Elements of Hindu Iconography*, Madras, 1914-15.

Rapson, E.J., Ed, *The Cambridge History of India*, Cambridge, 1921.

Rath, A. K., *Studies on Some Aspects of the History and Culture of Orissa*, Calcutta, 1987.

Rath, B.K., "An Unique Image of Chakreśvari," *O.H.R.J.*, Vol. XXIX, No.1-4(1978).

-------------, "Sculptural Art of Orissa", in H.C. Das, (Ed), *Cultural Heritage of Orissa.*

-------------, *Cultural History of Orissa*, New Delhi,1985.

-------------(Ed), *The Forgotten Monuments of Orissa*, 3 Vols., New Delhi, 1996.

Rawson, Philip, *The Art of Tantra,* Thames and Hudson, London, 1973.

Ray Choudhury, H.C., *Studies in Indian Antiquities*, Calcutta, 1958.

Ray P.K. (Ed), *A Report on Prachi Valley*, Orissa Sate Archaeology, Bhubaneswar, 1975.

Rowland, Benjamin, *The Art and Architecture of India*, Baltimore, 1953.

Sahai, B., *Iconography of Some Important Minor Hindu and Buddhist Deities*, New Delhi, 1975.

Sahu, J.K., *Historical Geography of Orissa*, New Delhi, 1997.

Sahu, N.K., "A Survey on the History of South Kosala", *N.A.H.O.*, Vol.I, 1971.

-------------, "New Light on Mahasivagupta Balarjuna*", O.H.R.J.*, Vol XXIII, 1978.

-------------, Odissa Itihas(Oriya),2.Vols, Cuttack,1987-88.

-------------, *Utkal University History of Orissa*, Vol.I, Bhubaneswar, 1964.

-------------, Misra, P.K. and Sahu J.K., *History of Orissa*, Cuttack, 1979.

Saraswati, S.K., "Temples of Orissa", *O.H.R.J.*, Vol I, 1953.

-------------, *A Survey of Indian Sculptures*, Cuttack, 1957.

Sastri,H.L., *South Indian Images of Gods and Goddesses*, Delhi,1974.

Shah, U.P., *Studies in Indian Art*, Bombay, 1955.

Sharma, B.K., *Somavaṁsī Rule in Orissa*, Calcutta, 1983.

Shukal, L.K., *A Study of Hindu Art and Architecture*, Varanasi, 1972.

Singh, Bahadur, *Brahmanical Icons in Northern India*, Sagar Publications, New Delhi,1977.

Singhdeo, J.P., *Cultural Profile of South Kosala*, New Delhi, 1987.

-------------, "Temples of Nawapara Subdivision", *O.H.R.J.*, Vol XXXIV, No.1-2.

Sinha, B.P., "Evolution of Śakti Worship in India", in D.C. Sircar (Ed), *The Śakti Cult and Tārā*, Calcutta, 1967.

Sircar, D. C., *The Śākta Pīṭhas*, Delhi, 1973.

-------------, *Select Inscriptions,* Calcutta, 1942.

-------------, *The Śākta Piṭhas Journal of the Royal Asiatic Society of Bengal*, Vol. XIV, No.1, 1948.

-------------,Studies *in the Geography of Ancient and Medieval India*, New Delhi, 1971.

Smith, V.A., *A History of Fine Art in India and Ceylone*, Oxford, 1930.

-------------, *Oxford History of India*, Oxford, 1920.

Srivastava, Balram, *Iconography of Śakti : A Study based on Śrītattvanidhi*, Varanasi, 1978.

Srivastava, M.C. P., *Mother Goddess in Indian Art, Archaeology and Literature*, Agam Kala Prakashan, Delhi, 1979.

Sterling, Andrew, "An Account, Geographical, Statistical and Historical of Orissa Proper or Cuttack" *A.R*, Vol. XV, 1822.

Subrahmanyam, R., *The Suryavaṁsī Gajapatis of Orissa*, Waltair, 1957.

-------------, *Inscriptions of the Suryavaṁsī Gajapatis of Orissa*, New Delhi, 1986.

Subudhi, U., *The Bhaumākaras of Orissa*, Calcutta, 1978.

Sukla, Ramadatta and Rutusila Sharma, (Ed.) *Navarātra Kalpataru* (Hindi),Allahabad, 1991.

-------------, *Durgā Kalpataru* (Hindi), Allahabad, 1984.

Tapasyananda, Swami, *Saundarya Lahari of Sri Sankaracarya*, Ramakrishna Math, Madras, 1987.

Tattwananda, Swami, *Vaisnava Sects, Śaiva Sects & Mother Worship*, Calcutta, 1984.

Thomas, P., *Epics, Myths and Legends of India*, Bombay, 1961.

Tiwari, A.N., *Orissa Review*, Monument Special, Cuttack, 1976.

Tiwari, J.N., *Goddess Cults in Ancient India*, Sandeep Prakashan, New Delhi, 1985.

Jagdish Narain Tiwari, Studies in Goddess Cults in Northern India, with Reference to the First Seven Centuries AD, Ph.D. diss,Australian National University.

Tiwari, S.P., *Comprehensive History of Orissa*, Calcutta, 1985.

-------------, *Hindu Iconography*, New Delhi, 1979.

Trivedi, Ramesh Datta, *Iconography of Pārvatī*, Delhi, 1981.

Tripathy,Snigdha, 'Ekāmra-Bhubanesvara',*O.H.R.J.*, Vol. XXXIII,no.1-2,1987.

Upadhyaya, Padma, *Female Images in the Museums of Utter Pradesh and their Social Background,* Chaukhambha Orientalia, Varanasi,1978

Vasu, Nagendra Nath, *The Archaelogical Survey of Mayurbhanja*,Vol.1, Calcutta, 1912.

Veronica Jons, *Indian Mythology*, *Ind Hamlyn*, London, 1967.

Vidyarthi, L.P., and B.K. Rai, *The Tribal Culture of India*, New Delhi, 1976.

Viennot, O., "The Goddess Mahiṣāsuramardinī in Kushana Art". *A.A.*, XIX, 1956.

Vogel, J. Ph., *Antiquities of Chamba State*, Calcutta, 1911.

-------------, *Indian Serbent Lore*, London, 1926

V.V. Bhide, *A Concise Sanskrit English Dictionary,* Chitrashala Press, Poona, 1926, p.868

Ward, W., *A view of the History, Religion and literature of Hindus*, Serampore, 1818.

Weiner Sheila, "From Gupta to Pala Sculpture", *A.A.*, Vol XXIV, 1962.

Whitehead,H., *Village Gods of Southern India*, Calcutta,1916.

Wilkins, W.J., *Hindu Mythology*, Indological Book House, Delhi, 1988.

Williams, M. Monier, *Sanskrit English Dictionary*, New Delhi, 2008.

Woodroff, John, *Śakti and Śākta*, 4th (Ed), Madras, 1951.

Wright, Thomas, 'Worship of the Generative Powers', *Sexual Symbolism*, New York, 1957.

Yocum, Glen, "The Goddess in a Tamil Śaiva Devotional", *Journal of the American Academy of Religion* 45, No.1, Supplement,1977.

Zimmer, Heinrich, *Myths and Symbols in Indian Art and Civilization* (Ed), Joseph Campbell, New York, 1962.

-------------, *The Art of Indian Asia* (Ed), Joseph Campbell, New York, 1955.

Journals

Annual Reports of the Archeological Survey of India, Ancient India, (Bulletin of the Archaeological Survey of India), New Delhi.

Asiatique Researches, Calcutta.

Bharati (Utkal University Research Journal), Bhubaneswar.

Bharati, A Bulletin of the Banaras Hindu University,Varanasi.

Bulletin of the School of Oriental Studies, London.

Chaṇḍī (Hindi), Allahabad, 1980-90.

Epigraphica Indica (Government of India Publication), New Delhi.

Indian Antiquary, Bombay.

Indian Culture, Calcutta.

Indian Historical Quarterly, Calcutta.

Jhankara (Odiya), Vol.37, 1985.

Journal of Ancient Indian History, Calcutta.

Journal of ancient Indian History, Trivandrum.

Journal of Ancient Society of Bengal (letters), Calcutta.

Journal of Ancient Society of Bengal, Calcutta.

Journal of Andhra Pradesh Historical Research Society, Rajmahendry.

Journal of Andhra the Historical Research Society.

Journal of Asiatic Society, Calcutta.

Journal of Bihar and Orissa Research Society, Bombay.

Journal of Bihar Research Society, Patna.

Journal of Kalinga Historical Research Society, Bolangir.

Journal of New Aspects on History of Orissa, P.G.Dept. History Sambalpur University.

Journal of Numismatic Society of India, Bombay.

Journal of Oriental Research, Madras.

Journal of Royal Society of Arts, London.

Kalyāṇa(Hindi), Gita press, Gorakhpur,1987.

Kosala through the Ages (Pamphlet No.2), Bolangir, 1947.

Memoirs of the Archaeological Survy of India, New Delhi.

New Aspects on History Of Orissa, P.G.Dept. History Sambalpur University.

Nirmalya (Oriya), Kacheri Road, Puri, issues from 1993-1995.

Orissa Historical Research Journal, Bhubaneswar.

Orissa Review, (Relevant issues).

Pr āchya Pratibhā, Bhopal.

Proceedings Of Indian History Congress,(Published from different places).

Proceedings Of Orissa History Congress,(Published from different places).

Saptarsi, Sambalpur University Journal.

Satayarsiki Smaranika, Sahitya Samiti, Khariar, 1983.

Srimandira (Oriya), Jagannath Mission, Puri, issues from 1990-1995

The Heritage, December, 1986.

The Koṇārk, Vol.36, 1978, Vol.39, 1979.

The Mirror, Vol.X, No.1, November, 1970.

Utkala Prasanga (Odiya).

Vijayā (Oriya), Madras and Bhubaneswar, November 1995.

Gazetteers

Behuria, N.C., *Orissa State Gazetteer*, Orissa State, 3.Vols, 1990-91

Bhatta, S.C., Ed., *The Encyclopaedic District Gazetteers of India*, Eastern Zone, Vol.9, New Delhi, 1997.

Senapati, N., and D.C. Kuanr, *Puri District Gazetteers*, Cuttack, 1977.

Senapati, N., Ed., *Orissa District Gazetteers,* Bolangir, 1968.

Senapati, N., Ed., *Baudh Kandhmal District Gazetteers*, Cuttack, 1983.

Senapati, N., Ed., *Bolangir District Gazetteers*, Cuttack, 1968.

Senapati, N., Ed., *Kalahandi District Gazetteers*, Cuttack, 1980.

Senapati, N., Ed., *Sambalpur District Gazetteers*, Cuttack, 1971.

Senapati, N., Ed., *Koraput District Gazetteers*, Cuttack, 1966.

Senapati, N., Ed., *Sundargarh District Gazetteers*, Cuttack, 1975.

Verma, Rajendra, Ed., *Madhya Pradesh District Gazetteers* (Relevant Volumes), Bhopal, 1973.

Pl.1. Alampur, Govt. Museum, A.P., Vaiṣṇavī, 7th century A.D.

Pl.2. Guntur, Chazeral, A.P., Vaiṣṇavī, 7th century A.D.

Pl.3 Tiruchchaturai, Tanjaur, Madras, Vaiṣṇavī, 9th century A.D.

Pl.4 Central Arch Museum, Gwalior, Vaiṣṇavī, 11th century A.D.

Pl.5 Seron Lalitpur,U.P., Vaiṣṇavī, 11th century A.D.

Pl.6 Tiruttani, Virattanesvara temple , Vaiṣṇavī, 12th century A.D.

Pl.7 Govt. Museum, Patna, Bihar, Vaiṣṇavī, 12th century A.D.

Pl.8 Bhubaneswar, Vaital deul, Vaiṣṇavī, 8th century A.D.

Pl.9 Belkhandi, Chandi temple, Vaiṣṇavī, 10th century A.D.

Pl.10 Daśāśvamedhaghāṭ: Jājaur, Vaiṣṇavī,10th century A.D.

Pl.11 Sathalapura: Vaiṣṇavī,11th century A.D.

Pl. 12 Dharnaśala: Vaiṣṇavī,11th century A.D.

Pl.13 Khicing: Mayurbhanja ,Vaiṣṇavī, 11th century A.D.

Pl. 14 Dia: Narayani Temple, Khurda, Vaiṣṇavī, 14th century A.D.

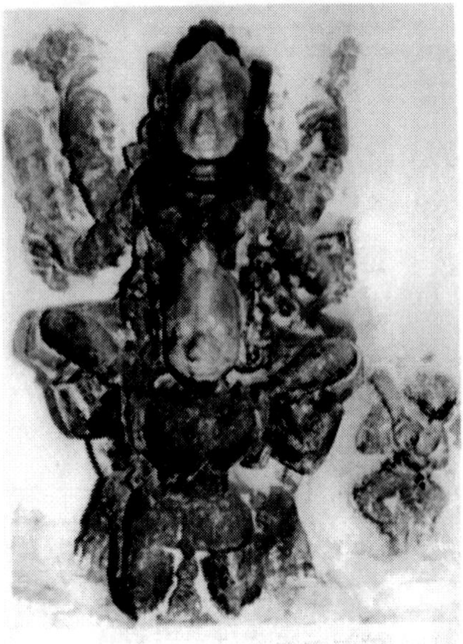

Pl.15 Sonepur: Samalai Temple, Vaiṣṇavī, 18th century A.D.

Pl.16 Gujurata:, Vaiṣṇavī Saptamātṛkā panel, 18th century A.D.

Pl.17 National Museum, Delhi, Saptamātṛkā, 8th century A.D.

Pl.18 Govt.Museum, Mathura, Saptamātṛkā, 9th century A.D.

Pl.19 Sathalapura, Odisha, Saptamātṛkā, 10th century A.D.

Pl. 20 Ranipur-Jharial: Odisha, Saptamātṛkā, 10th century A.D.

Pl.21 State Museum, Lucknow, Saptamātṛkā, 11th century A.D.

INDEX

A

B

C

D